Live Happily Ever After

By Steve Johnson

Cover design by David C Johnson

Live Happily Ever After ...

Moving beyond fairytales to claim the relationship you never imagined possible.

By Steve Johnson

Author of the relationship assessment

www.LiveHappilyEverAfter.com

Copyright 2019 Next Generation WI LLC
All rights reserved.

Table of Contents

Dedication 7

Introduction 9

Chapter 1: COMMUNICATION 22

Chapter 2: COMPANIONSHIP 53

Chapter 3: CONFIDANT 80

Chapter 4: CONSUMMATE 101

Chapter 5: COMMITMENT 132

Dedication

This book would be completely impossible without my wife, Lynne. We met when we were in high school and began a friendship that grew to become the defining relationship in our lives. We were both naïve about what marriage was all about. We had never seen a relationship that was the standard we were hoping to have. We knew one thing, we loved each other.

Love is essential, but as you read this book you will see how patient and kind Lynne was. I was a slow learner. We weren't "perfect" for each other, but over the years were "perfected" for each other.

Lynne is a lovely woman, beautiful on the inside and out. She has blossomed from the girl I met at 16, to being an amazing wife, mother and grandmother. Professionally, leaders from all over the country seek out her advice through a consulting company she started and leads called 2xConsulting.com.

As we grew, we made sure that we grew together. Lynne often made the biggest sacrifices, and she wouldn't have wanted it any other way. She is the most amazing woman that I have ever met. After 42 years of marriage, I am more in love with her today than ever before.

This book chronicles what we have learned, and have often shared with others, to help them grow their relationship. Lynne is a woman of wisdom, and often as we were meeting with a couple, I would marvel at her ability to find just the right words to help guide a couple toward greater intimacy.

Lynne, I love you. Thank you for being my partner on this journey called life. You have helped me grow and become the man I am today. I can't imagine my life without you.

Although you didn't write the words of this book, it could never have been written without the wisdom that I have gained from watching your life, listening to your words and experiencing your love daily. Thank you for being my wife and sharing your life with me.

Introduction

Most everyone I've ever met is looking for a relationship with another person that can grow from friendship to romance and finally to the defined, committed relationship which lasts the rest of their lives.

For most of us, it's an oddity to long for what we've never seen growing up. From the time of understanding, I never saw the passion that must have once existed in the relationship between my parents. What is the impact of growing up in a home like mine? What is the real possibility of "falling in love"?

I don't like the phrase "Live Happily Ever After" very much, but most people, even in a world filled with the carnage of broken relationships, hold out hope that there is that one person with whom they could meet, fall in love and defy the odds.

My purpose in writing this book is to share with you some good news. I've experienced this in my personal life and also as a pastor who has officiated at well over 500 weddings. The good news is you can find and develop a relationship with a person where there is true love.

Love is wonderful and vulnerable. That is why I am writing this book. I want to share important decisions that you can make to "Live Happily Ever After."

You may have never seen an example of the relationship that you long for. You may have fallen prey to a marriage that ended in divorce. In writing this, I want to share that there is hope. You can believe in love; it is neither a fairytale nor is it a tall tale. It is a lot of work and learning, but I truly want you to believe in love and believe that a lifelong passionate relationship is possible for you.

I grew up in a home where my parents stayed married because of their five children. Divorce was less acceptable than it is today, and although I had every reason not to believe that a love relationship was possible, that all changed when I met a girl in high school who was everything I could have hoped for. We started by growing a friendship and from that friendship, feelings emerged that were foreign to me, unlike anything I had ever felt or seen expressed before. I had never met such a truly authentic, caring, kind, talented, hardworking girl before, whose beauty emerged from the depths of her heart. I remember telling a friend after meeting her, "I could marry a girl like her."

Little did I know that 44 years after meeting her, we would be celebrating our 42nd wedding anniversary and that my passion for her today is far greater than when we began our journey together. She is not the same girl I met; she has grown and matured and has become more than I could have ever imagined. And I'm sure I'm not the same person that she met either. She was willing to take a huge risk in making a commitment of her life to me. You might think "what was the risk?" or "you seemed perfect for each other," but neither was true.

First, there is no such thing as a perfect person or relationship. Over years of trying our best, making mistakes, and asking for forgiveness, we have been "perfected" for each other. The process has not been easy, but it has been worth it. There were times that I was frustrated with myself or Lynne or just the circumstances of our lives. Sometimes I couldn't figure out why I was unhappy. What was even more challenging was trying to figure out why she wasn't happy.

If you are looking for the perfect person to share your life with, stop looking. I'm afraid that person doesn't exist. If you are willing to be discriminating in who you allow into your life, and grow from friendship toward a committed relationship, you can become "perfected" for each other. This requires acknowledgment, from the very beginning of your relationship, that both of you value the other so much that you are committed to change and growth.

What is the reason 50% of marriages end, and of the remaining, most are nothing more than utilitarian? It is because those couples weren't willing to be "perfected" for their partner. A great deal of effort is needed by both people to defy the odds; but it can be done, and I want to help you.

Here is a personal observation after many years of counseling with hundreds of couples. For most, the greatest effort is put into their relationship prior to the wedding. Many hours and a great amount of resources are put into the wedding day to make it just perfect. The venue, the dresses, the flowers, the cake, the music...everything is just the way the couple wants it...for **one** day. If only that effort and investment continued into the years to follow, they too would defy the odds and define for friends and family, what marriage was truly intended to be.

The emerging generation does have cause to fear marriage. To many, "a piece of paper" means little. They want to test-drive a relationship first to see if it works. I certainly can understand the reasoning, but sadly I have read there is a higher divorce rate among couples who live together prior to marriage. It appears that taking a test-drive doesn't really work. Instead, a couple needs to take the steps described in this book to truly be committed to making your relationship prosper. I do know there are some couples who have taken a "test-drive" and have a happy, successful relationship, but it is a very small percentage.

In many ways it defies logic, but it appears statistically correct, that you need to define your relationship first, and then do the hard work daily, if you want to have a successful relationship. Many of the areas addressed in this book are bedrock principles that get overlooked when you test drive your relationship. It would be like taking a half-built car out for a test drive and expecting it to run perfectly. The odds that you would return it to the dealership are high. Please take the time necessary to build a strong basis for your relationship before jumping in to a less than ready relationship.

My purpose in writing this book is not to pile guilt on those who have gone through a broken relationship. Instead I would like to offer hope to those who truly want a relationship that will last a lifetime by sharing with you what I have personally experienced. As a flawed man, who has enjoyed an intimate, passionate, best friend relationship with Lynne for over 42 years, and as a pastor who has invested great effort in preparing couples for marriage over the last 40 years, I want to share some personal insights I have gained.

You might wonder whether this will be relevant to living in our modern world with hook ups and technology driving relationships. I promise you that what you are looking for is the same thing that your parents, grandparents and great grandparents were looking for. The fashion, music and technology may be different, but the internal desire to share your life with someone is no different and the means necessary to build an intimate relationship hasn't changed either. You deserve this. I hope that the journey this book will take you through will help you to better understand what is necessary to defy the odds. I have allowed you to see my vulnerabilities telling you the biggest mistakes that I have made in learning to be husband. I don't want to pretend to have it all together, because I don't. Even while writing this I have been reminded of areas that I need to work on.

So, join me on this journey and experience new possibilities that are waiting for you in a committed relationship.

There are initial stages in any relationship, like attraction and chemistry, which trigger those first, fluttery feelings. What is even more thrilling is that I'm more in love with Lynne today than I could have ever imagined 42 years ago. I still remember telling her, "I love you," for the first time. I was so nervous. I thought, what happens if she says, "That's nice." It took courage for me to share my feelings with her, and it continues to take courage to deepen our relationship. I was so thankful that she responded in kind. At that moment, I couldn't have imagined anything more profound, but through the years I have learned that those early affirmations of love were just planting seeds in the soil of our relationship that would need to be tended. Weeds would need to be pulled and seasons of drought would need to be addressed. There wasn't an automatic pilot we could turn on and have our relationship grow. We chose to focus on our relationship and say "no" to even good things to protect our time or energy for our relationship. I wish I could tell you that we have had the perfect marriage, but I can't. I shared earlier that the best we can hope for is a "perfected" marriage. I am very happy with a continually "perfecting" relationship with my bride. It makes me excited about our future.

If you go to the courthouse, purchase a marriage license, sign your names as husband and wife, in the presence of an officiant, you are making the largest emotional, financial and spiritual commitment of your entire life. Think about it. Your names, two witness signatures, filed with the clerk of courts and you have either made the best decision of your life or the worst decision of your life. In just a few moments, two people who were thinking about the happiness of the present, can take a wrong turn into the future, because they aren't thinking of the long-term effort, commitment and time which is needed to insure a great relationship.

A strong, committed relationship is not luck. It is hard work and a willingness to make changes, to allow your partner and yourself to become all that is intended. In this context, with your relationship always on the forefront, you can live happily ever after. "Happy" might not necessarily be the best word, because happiness is so dependent upon current circumstances and there can be very challenging seasons in every relationship. Perhaps words like satisfied, contented, pleased, and passionate are more realistic.

We are very proud grandparents. We love our grandchildren and see the extraordinary effort required of our son and daughter-in-law in rearing them. The same work we did in raising our children has faded a bit from our memory. Love during this season means being a team that can't wait to sleep together, and I truly mean SLEEP! There is a still a growing passion, but it might express itself in a different way during sleepless nights and lack of privacy.

I'm writing this book to be open and honest. I'd love for you to learn from the mistakes I made. One of the keys to our success is I owned my mistakes; I owned it and asked for forgiveness. I never lost sight of what I wanted our relationship to become. Lynne followed the same path. Neither of us had witnessed the relationship we longed for, so we knew there would be trial and error along the way, and that both of us needed to be humble and forgiving.

This book is going to take you on a journey to the essential parts of a successful relationship.

I have a tool called "Live Happily Ever After" which is an assessment giving your insight into the very areas you will be reading about. (www.LiveHappilyEverAfter.com) this is a tool designed for couples to use at least once a year. Taking it in the early stages of your relationship will help both of you understand what it takes to have a great relationship. In a matter of a year our lives change so much, that taking this assessment will give you quantitative information on your relationship and whether it is moving forward or if there is an area that you are struggling with. There are five broad areas measured, along with three sub-categories under each of the five. You receive a combined quantitative score in each sub-category and an overall composite score. When each of you honestly answers the questions, the computer combines your individual results into one cumulative report.

Once I wrote this assessment, my wife and I were the first to take it. After answering the questions and getting the report, it showed us specifically what was holding us back in having our greatest relationship. Neither of us felt blamed, since it is a combined report. It turned out, that we both were feeling unsatisfied in the same areas. We now could create an action plan to work on the specific areas that we wanted to improve. What we discovered is that by knowing what to work on, the satisfaction of our entire relationship grew. We take this evaluation every six months.

We have made the price of this relationship inventory affordable so that couples would not have any financial burden in constantly monitoring their relationship. I hope that you would take the evaluation even as you are reading this book. In the chapters to follow, I will discuss what I have learned about the five broad and fifteen sub areas that I believe are critical in fulfilling the desires you have in your relationship.

I want you to defy the odds and be "perfected" for each other. I want you to know all of the joy and passion that comes as you make your relationship a priority. With focused hard work and careful evaluation of your ever-changing relationship, you can set the goal to "Live Happily Ever After."

Enjoy this book. It has taken 42 years to write. I would also encourage you to take the evaluation found at www.LiveHappilyEverAfter.com and review the results with your spouse or committed partner. I only wish Lynne and I would have had this tool, and the information in this book, when we were about to get married. We have learned many lessons the hard way. My goal for you is that you can get a head start as a result of what we have learned.

Chapter 1: COMMUNICATION

The first broad area that we will discuss is communication. Countless couples have come into my office to tell me about their relationship and how they've fallen in love. I ask them what the best part of their relationship is and almost always they tell me how easy it is to talk with one another.

The ability to communicate is absolutely essential in a successful relationship. Often times, the same couple will come back to me a few years later, because they are unhappy with their relationship. When I ask why, their response is just the opposite of what they previously shared with me...we just can't seem to communicate!

I would say that communication is the hardest area of a relationship to keep growing. Great communication means that the thoughts and perspective of one person, given their gender, experience, and background, needs to be received by another person given their gender, experience, and background. The couple may be able to hear the same words, but words carry different meanings depending on our background. In addition, when we speak, we use a certain "tone." This multiplies the difficulty in understanding each other.

When people first start a relationship, their conversations are very affirming. They don't require the complexity of communication as it pertains to paying bills or deciding household responsibilities. A couple overestimates how good they are at communication before marriage, and then aren't quite sure how to handle miscommunication. It is very important that couples understand that they each speak a foreign dialect.

Life offers so many distractions today. Often a person will feel compelled to look at their digital device even during a date night. All of the new ways to communicate has actually dumbed down our ability to sit and talk. Sharing our hopes, dreams and fears isn't accomplished in a text with an emoji. Technology is amazing, but you can't snuggle with it at night. Passion is sustained by deep communication that is done the old fashion way; face to face, looking into other's eyes and sharing your hearts with each other.

After Lynne and I met, I was given her address and because she lived 100 miles from me, I wrote her a letter… with real paper and a pen. I had to address the envelope, put a stamp on it and send it off. We wrote most every day and still have all the letters in a special container. Lynne's mother was the postal carrier for their home. I certainly increased her workload, and I'm sure she was wondering about this guy who was writing her daughter every day. In our bedroom today we have framed the envelopes containing the first letters we wrote to each other. I know that the year of writing most every day started a pattern of communication that has helped us throughout our 42 years of marriage.

At that time, you had to pay for long distance calls. Any call outside of the city you lived in was expensive. I remember waiting until it was the cheapest time to call, just to hear her voice. Today, most people have cellphones with unlimited text and calling. I'm actually glad that those phone calls cost me something. It made me value each conversation and made it hard to hang up. To this day if I am away from Lynne, I still call, just to hear her voice several times a day. I want to hear her voice. I'm not a fan of texting. I do it when necessary, but I can tell so much from the tone of her voice and the words that she chooses. We also end even very short calls with the words, "I love you." In my professional life I have made it clear to anyone that I'm meeting with that if my wife, children or now grandchildren call, I am going to answer it. I not only want to hear their voices, but I also want to create expectations for my wife, children and grandchildren that communicating with them is very important to me. It's not often that I have to interrupt a meeting with a call from one of them, but after I hang up from the call, most people tell me that they are going to start doing the same thing.

No relationship can become successful without gaining high levels of skill in communication. Without this you have no relationship at all. Couples who fail to invest in this area, or simply think that their skills will never atrophy, will one day wake up and not know the person that they once thought they knew. Communication is essential. It is bedrock. This is the starting place to improve your relationships. What once was so natural and easy may have become short answers or grunts as you leave each other and go on with your daily routine. Communication was never meant to simply be utilitarian. It is the vehicle through which our hearts meet and stay connected.

In our technology-rich society, we have actually lost some of our ability to communicate. One of five broad areas that build a relationship is communication. The sub areas are what make true communication possible. So, follow along with me as we explore the sub areas of this important category. It is here that Lynne and I made a major discovery about our relationship. We were failing until we took the evaluation, Live Happily Ever After. More about that later.

If I were to give one piece of advice, it would be to offer a positive assumption to your partner when listening to what they say. If you assume the best, you will most often discover that the best was intended.

Now we move on to three skills that need to be learned to be successful in communication.

1. Active Listening

When you first think about listening, you think it is perhaps a passive experience, but that is not the type of listening that strengthens communications. Listening is one of the most important skills anyone can learn, and then refine. While you are listening, you are allowing all of your concentration to be directed at the person who is communicating with you. When you refine this skill, you are able to understand certain nuances of the person speaking and gain great insight into the depth of what is being discussed.

Active listing involves more than paying close attention. It is taking responsibility to ask questions and clarify the person's meaning when it's not clear to you. Successful communication is the shared responsibility of the speaker and the listener. The goal is to thoroughly understand the essence of what is being communicated. Active listening might mean you move closer to hear or see the other person better. It means letting a person finish a thought before you interrupt. It means trying to understand what they are saying even if you might have chosen different words. As a listener try not to critique but try to understand. If you concern yourself with listening, then you will learn the individual dialect of that person which will help you in future conversations.

Use all of your energy to pay attention to word choice, tone, and facial expressions with the goal of understanding. At an appropriate pause, summarize to the person what you believe you have heard and ask for any clarification.

This area has been a struggle for me. My mind is active and often times I make assumptions about what the person is going to say and my mind drifts. This is a skill that I have worked hard on and still have a long way to go. My wife Lynne on the other hand has amazing listening skills. I watch how she interacts with people and often people comment on how much they enjoy their conversations with her. She pays close attention, gives physical cues that she is completely focused, and asks questions about areas that the person is clearly passionate about. Lynne has been a great example to me.

The Center for Creative Leaders has published 7 key active listening skills. They are as follows:

1) Be attentive

2) Ask open-ended questions

3) Ask probing questions

4) Request clarification

5) Paraphrase

6) Be attuned to and reflect feelings

7) Summarize

From the list above, you can see that becoming an excellent active listener is not an easy task. It requires not only knowledge, but also the discipline to implement the knowledge into your conversations.

Practice, practice, practice. I need to remind myself before each conversation that I am committed to truly mastering the skill of active listening. For some people this comes naturally, but either way it has to become a reality in your life. Without these skills you will limit every relationship that you have, but most importantly you won't properly hear the person you are in a committed relationship with.

The assessment tool, Live Happily Ever After® will measure each of the areas we are discussing in this book. You receive a combined relationship score in each area. This is one of the keys to unlocking true intimacy. If you gain the skills of an active listener, you will discover that every conversation will mean more, and that people will be drawn to you because you show your interest in them, not by your words, but by your listening skills. The power of listening can't be overstated.

Helpful Hints:

- One of the most difficult and most valuable skills to learn is active listening. This means that you are fully engaged with your eyes and ears. No devices turned on! We have to manage our social media time carefully so that it doesn't impact our most important relationships. No one can multitask if your goal is growing an intimate relationship. As a sign of respect, put down your phone and put it face down. Turn the volume off and give your partner your full attention.

• Let your partner speak without interrupting and work at asking questions that draw out more of what he or she is thinking on the subject.

• Often times, your partner just wants to be listened to, so don't interrupt. Interrupting short-circuits the process and doesn't allow you to hear what is going on deep in their heart.

• When your partner shares a problem with you, don't feel the need to fix the problem. Just listen, be understanding and compassionate.

• Active listening is one of the least developed skills in most relationships. If you can master this skill, it will have a huge impact on your relationship.

2. Verbally engaged

The second skill that must be developed to become a master at communication is being verbally engaged. Because you have grown as an active listener, you will have appropriate comments related to the issues that you concentrated on. It is important in a conversation that it is a shared experience. Your task is to master the skills of verbal communication. Even if you are a quiet person, YOUR words are essential.

I married a100% Swedish woman. Swedish men have the reputation of using few words. I heard a story of a Swedish man who was asked by his wife why he didn't tell her more often that he loved her. His response was, "I told you I loved you the day we got married. If anything changes, I'll let you know." Yikes!

When we first were married, my wife was a woman of very few words. I'm not sure if it was the culture she grew up in, or if she was just shy. As she has grown, she's become a brilliant communicator, but still tends to be on the quiet side. This caused problems in our early marriage because I needed affirmation that I was a good husband and was meeting her needs. I had to explain to her that I couldn't understand her unless she talked to me. This is a skill that everyone can learn. It is essential if you are married or in a committed relationship. No one is a mind reader and if you force someone to be one, your relationship will suffer.

This doesn't mean talking without filtering. All of us must "own" our words. We must discipline ourselves to choose the correct words that are best understood by others. With our spouse we should become experts at what words comfort, inspire, affirm and gain awareness of those that hurt. The spoken word is very powerful. Once the words leave our lips, they can never be unheard.

When you discover that a word choice was hurtful, make note of it and don't use it again. Excellent communication means that your word choices are fully understood by the listener. It's not only word choice, but timing. Sometimes your partner may be caring for children, about to leave for work or ready to go to sleep. Those situations limit our communication, so be careful with your word choices and the subjects you bring up.

Find the best time to talk about difficult subjects and use words that don't escalate tension. When you see this happening, pull back and ask for forgiveness, and either rephrase your thoughts or suggest another time to talk about that subject.

I have known couples that use the silent treatment as a punishment. One couple told me that they had gone two weeks without saying a word unless it was absolutely necessary. How foolish! If our words have caused a problem, the only solution is to use words to correct the problem. Wasting weeks trying to punish the person you love the most, punishes you just as much, and causes increased separation every time it is done.

If you have worked on active listening, you have the advantage of becoming an excellent verbal communicator. You can add to the conversation in a healthy way which allows you to be better understood.

If you want to "Live Happily Ever After," you must learn the art of verbal communication. Some people find opening up and talking very difficult. They tend to answer with as few words as possible. There can be many reasons why they do that. Most people speak much more than they listen. Both modes of communication need to be balanced, so ultimate understanding can be experienced. It is essential in a committed relationship that both share ample words to participate in an ongoing conversation. Both parties need to have the ability to share their hopes, dreams, fears and love for one another. For many, this level of vulnerability is very difficult, but is essential. Take small steps if necessary but open up your life. Share with the most trusted person in your life. If they have worked on active listening, they will respond appropriately and welcome each word you speak.

There are many couples that find it hard to say the words "I love you." When they come to me with concerns about their relationship, I ask them to sit facing each other with knees touching and while looking into each other's eyes say "I love you" four times. You would think I was pulling their teeth by the expressions that they give me. The first time is hard. Often there will be an awkward chuckle or eyes that glance away while they do their assignment.

I then require them to say those powerful words at least four times each day. I would ask them immediately when they returned for our next meeting if they had fulfilled their assignment, and often, they would have to do some quick catchups in front of me. It might sound silly to you, but these words should always flow often and easily, and should never be withheld. Once it becomes easy with your spouse, you will find it becomes easier with other important people in your life.

I can't remember my father ever saying, "I love you." My mother lavished her children with those words. With our own children, we spoke these words often. Now as adults, every email, text, call or conversation includes those precious words. As a grandparent, I want my grandchildren to understand how important those words are. They are very free in telling us of their love. It fills our hearts. They have learned the importance by our example, in the hundreds of times they have heard it spoken directly from our lips.

Being verbally engaged requires that you are not only an active listener, but that you are willing to work at developing knowledge about what is important to those to whom you are committed. If you are having a difficult time conversing, it might be because you have no overlap in shared interests. It is an opportunity to enrich your life by learning about the career or hobbies of your spouse.

I grew up in Green Bay Wisconsin. If you grow up in Green Bay, you bleed green and gold. For those of you who don't know what I'm talking about, I'm referring to the Green Bay Packers. A city of just over 100,000 people has one of the most well-known and storied Pro Football teams of all time. The stadium holds 84,441 seats. The waiting list has 115,000 people hoping for season tickets. When a child is born in Green Bay, the parents immediately put them on the waiting list with the hopes that when they are in their 30's, they will get the opportunity to own season tickets. The last time a game was not sold out was on November 22, 1959 when 297 tickets went unsold.

All this to say that when Lynne married me and moved to Green Bay while I was finishing my undergraduate degree, she was in for a culture shock. She knew very little about the game, but she quickly realized that if she was going to have a conversation with anyone in Green Bay, she had to understand the game. She became a quick learner and even though this wasn't a natural interest of hers, she cheered louder than I did. We moved to Minneapolis a couple years later where I started graduate school. I think there was a bit of relief that she could talk about more than the "Green and Gold."

I had to take the same responsibility. It was important that what she cared about, I cared about. Lynne went on to become a school teacher. She taught both first and fourth grades. Each week I would bring healthy treats to her classroom and read to her students. She was so busy as a teacher … I don't think most people realize how hard teachers work. I would add a little fun to her classroom by building a tepee and a huge igloo made of plastic milk jugs hot glued together. Lynne used them both as a special place for silent reading. The igloo eventually became an underwater sea cave when her ocean theme came along, complete with clear, blue wrap. How fun it was!

You might not live in Green Bay or be married to a school teacher, but you can allow your lives to intersect more than just at home. One of my favorite memories was when Lynne was enrolled in graduate school and on the first day of class, she became ill. She thought about cancelling the class, but instead I went to the first class for her. When the professor handed out the syllabus, took roll of the students and called Lynne Johnson, I said, "Here." The professor said, "You are Lynne Johnson?" I explained the situation and found the class so interesting that I kept asking questions. At the end of the class period, the professor asked me if I'd like to just sit in on the rest of the semester. I had a great time. I learned a lot, and I even debated back and forth with this wonderful professor. Lynne would sometimes hang her head, but I wasn't being graded and the professor loved having an interested student in the 2 ½ hour class. Being verbally engaged means that you care enough to learn about your spouse's life and can talk intelligently about things you would have never otherwise learned. Lynne has always jumped in feet first in new adventures I've taken. This has kept our relationship interesting and fun to be around each other.

I believe that some new forms of communication have actually cheapened what it means to communicate. We have had to discipline ourselves to silence our phone and turn them face down in order to not be overwhelmed by all of the other communication that can steal away time from the most important person in my life. If this is an area that you have struggled in, and if you aren't sure what to talk about, then find ways of intersecting your lives in multiple areas. You might discover that you are very interested in areas that you never even thought of.

One last thought… take risks to share the hopes, dream and fears that you have. If your spouse is a good active listener, they will welcome this, and you will grow in intimacy. There is no one I would rather spend time with than Lynne. If we hadn't worked so hard at active listening and verbal communication, I'm not sure this would be true. Be diligent at this, and I guarantee it will pay off big time.

Helpful Hints:

- Each person speaks a foreign language. We might use the same words, but based upon our age, where we grew up, education, etc. we need to understand that true communication takes place when the person listening is able to understand what is said. Approach what you say in a way where you are making a real effort at being understood. During a conversation, ask if you were clear or if there seems to be confusion. Then ask your partner to re-state what you said. It's important that you don't become defensive on this point. If we approach the fact that our language is foreign to our partner, then we can expect misunderstandings and work harder at being clear.

- Watch the intensity of the words that you choose. If you are discussing a problem area in your relationship, be careful not to use words that could make the situation worse. Gentle words are going to get your point across in a way that your partner won't take offense.
- A good rule of thumb would be to say 10 affirming comments to your partner for every 1 comment that could be perceived as negative.
- Ask your partner if there are certain words or phrases that are offensive to them and try to always choose other words or phrases. We each have a history and often that history has some hurts. Those hurts can be triggered by past use of certain words or phrases. Be very careful to build a positive vocabulary that can be shared in your relationship. You are creating your own collective dialect.
- When your partner is talking with you, stop whatever you are doing and give them your complete attention. As you are in the

process of creating a personal dialect, ask for clarification and try to find common words to communicate similar thoughts.

• Talk about things that bring you joy as individuals and as a couple. Find ways of focusing on shared interests.

3. Understanding

The third sub-area measured by the tool, "Live Happily Ever After" is understanding each other. What is the purpose of being an active listener and having skills in being verbally engaged if it isn't to understand each other? Do I have a story for you!!

I mentioned earlier that as a pastor, I officiated at well over 500 weddings. I would meet with the couple for hours to prepare them for marriage and then after 3 months, I had a mandatory "checkup" with them. I really wanted them well prepared for this new level of commitment in their relationship. I loved every minute of the time I spent with each couple. Lynne would often be involved in these sessions and was always welcomed. She had great insights.

I also spent time each week getting emergency phone calls from couples that thought their marriage was over and wanted to meet with me. Thankfully most of these relationships not only survived but also prospered. We all need a check up on the core areas of our relationship to find out how we are doing.

After Lynne and I were married for 38 years, I went online to find an evaluation that we could take to let us know how we were doing. I couldn't find anything. So, I decided with the experience I had, I would write a marriage assessment that became Live Happily Ever After. (www.LiveHappilyEverAfter.com)

After many years of meeting with couples, it was pretty easy for me to list the categories that should be included in this tool, and to write questions in each area. After it was all completed, I contacted one of my closest friends, Dave Jaworski, who was an early employee at Microsoft. Dave is brilliant and writes computer code in nine languages. I told him what I had done and asked him if he would write the code. He agreed and sent Lynne and me the first codes to test the evaluation. Lynne and I had worked hard on our relationship from dating through, at that time, 38 years of marriage. I learned that if your marriage is fulfilling, the rest of the world can be crumbling around you, and you can still be happy.

We took the evaluations and the results were positive ... well mostly positive. When you take the evaluation, there are five broad categories and three subcategories for each broad category. Communication being a broad category had Active Listening, Verbal Engagement and Understanding Each Other as the subcategories. We scored in the 90's in all of the categories listed in the evaluation except Understanding Each Other. Our combined score was 60 ... that is an "F"!! We had worked so hard at listening and talking to each other, what could possibly cause us to both answer the questions in a way that gave us such a low score in understanding each other. We were baffled!

The following week, I had scheduled an executive physical at Mayo Clinic. I had a friend who had gone through the program and really believed I would benefit from a three-day thorough physical. Mayo Clinic is amazing. Every aspect of my care exceeded anything I had ever experienced before. I first met with a physician who took a health history. He then set up a three-day test schedule including a stress test, blood tests, dermatology etc., and as the results would come in, more tests would pop up on my schedule. I was looking at my packed three-day schedule and saw audiology was up next. I wondered why they added that test. I met with the audiologist and said I wasn't certain why I was seeing them and was assured it was just routine. When I finished my hearing exam, the Doctor went over the results with me. Without any previous awareness, I discovered that I only had 50% of normal hearing. Live Happily Ever After scored us 60% at understanding each other, and now I understood why. I was actually told that my greatest hearing loss was in the higher tones that most women speak in. I probably was the only person happy to hear that they had lost 50% of their hearing, because our mystery had been solved.

The reason why we scored poorly at understanding each other was because I didn't hear much of what was being said. Like most couples, we had developed some bad habits like talking between walls or talking while the other person was walking away. I was so glad that there was an explanation to our score of 60. I got hearing aids, and we changed our bad habits with communication so that most of the time we are looking at each other and trying to avoid talking between walls. While we still struggle at times when we are being lazy, I am happy that we could improve this area of our relationship.

The next time we took the assessment (we take it every six months), our score went from 60 to the 90's. I have often wondered what I had missed during the season that our score was 60. If you take the assessment, and score lower than you expect in one area, be open to the idea that it might be a physical issue.

I shared earlier that every person has their own unique language or dialect. To grow in intimacy, each of us have to learn a foreign language. It honors our partner to take the time to understand them, and not correct them. They may never *speak* in our dialect, but if they understand it and we understand theirs, true communication can take place.

Often couples have come to me because they can't get over an argument about an area of their relationship. I will meet with them together and then each separately. Next, I have them come back together with me, and most of the time I will phrase in slightly different words, what I heard from both of them. Usually they say in unison, "That's what I mean!" Here they thought they disagreed about an issue that became so big they made an appointment with me, only to discover that they completely agreed with each other, but struggled to understand each other without my involvement. If you find yourself in that situation, please try to give a positive assumption to your spouse, and if necessary, then find someone you trust to help you better understand what they mean.

Be open to new ideas or perspectives on different subjects. A healthy relationship means that you are constantly learning and benefiting from your partner's personal growth. You may come to different sides on an issue, but that will make you better understand the other side. Too often we surround ourselves exclusively with people who hold exactly our same opinions. You don't want to be caught in that trap. Life is far bigger than your current experiences, and knowledge is being added at an escalating rate. New ideas should always be welcome. They may not change your opinion on a subject, but they will make you a more interesting person.

Helpful Hints:

- Communication is one of the most challenging parts of any relationship. This is often the case because we assume that our partner understands the full depth and meaning of the words we say. Recognize the difficulty and you will be inspired to see it as a challenge rather than an obstacle.
- Take responsibility when you are talking to phrase your conversation in a way that your partner will best understand, and then ask them if they have any questions.

- Take the time to develop a special vocabulary as a couple. These words can be playful, romantic or very serious. Taking the time to make sure that you have a shared vocabulary will allow you to get understanding when either of you are quickly trying to get your point across.

- Include your partner in areas of your life that he or she doesn't share. Describe, for example, your career and key definitions so that they can better understand what you mean when you use your work vocabulary. If your goal is to grow in intimacy, you can't leave out your career, which often absorbs more time than you have with each other.

Summary thoughts about Communication:

I believe that this is an essential area of growth for every couple ... including my wife and me. We are always learning and experiencing new things, and if we aren't careful our separate dialects will make communication more difficult.

Some people believe that women speak far more than men, and some do. But James Pennebaker, chair of the University of Texas at Austin's psychology department, says he was skeptical of the lopsided stats when he saw them quoted in an interview with Louann Brizendine in *The New York Times Magazine*. "I read that and knew it couldn't be true simply because we've run too many studies," he says, "it just didn't make sense." In fact, he had been collecting data over the past decade with colleagues at the University of Arizona in Tucson that specifically showed that the sexes are about equal when it comes to a war of words.

There are some extremes on both ends with some speaking as little as 500 words per day and at the other end some speaking up to 47,000 words each day. I wouldn't want to be at ether extreme. What was discovered by Dr. Pennebaker is that women speak an average of 16,215 words and men 15,669. Statistically almost identical. However, the subjects varied drastically where women spoke mostly about people or relationships and men about objects.

If you want to grow together in communication, then together you need to focus on subjects that build your relationship. This will create a place of safety and intimacy that if continued, will allow your "Live Happily Ever After" scores to reflect your hard work.

Chapter 2:
COMPANIONSHIP

One of the greatest parts of being in a committed relationship is having companionship. We live in a fast-paced world that has redefined the word "friend" by Facebook. Facebook is the amazing tool to help keep track of people in your life, but has also diminished the term "friend" to an extremely low level. You may have 1,000 "friends" on Facebook and still live a lonely life.

When you meet a person and grow to love them, you want to upgrade the definition of the word "friend." That special person becomes a redefinition of every relationship you've ever had. In a committed relationship, the goal is that it would last a lifetime.

When Lynne and I got married, I was 21 and she was 19. I felt like such an "adult" that I had no trouble making a lifelong commitment, but to be honest I didn't have a clue to what that meant. We had never seen a marriage relationship that we wanted to model ours after, but all I knew is I wanted to spend as many minutes of the day with this incredible woman as I could. I was willing to learn from my mistakes and had set the goal of being the best husband that she could ever have. I'm sure that I have failed her many times, but the goal remains.

Getting married that young, meant that our lives would be busy. As I look back, too busy. I had to finish college and then graduate school. A year after we were married, we happily discovered that our family was going to grow, so I took a fulltime job working 3-11:30 p.m. and went to school during the day. Between work, school and homework, I was completely oblivious to the fact that I didn't have time to breathe, let alone honor my marriage vow to be her companion. Our son was born and that kept her very busy. She was and is a wonderful mother. If you asked her, even though she has had an incredible career, she would tell you she was born to be a mother and grandmother.

I didn't take the time to consider what her life was like. I just tried to survive finishing college and paying the bills, and in retrospect,

I think that I failed her greatly. She must have been so lonely. As grandparents, I see how hard my son and daughter-in-law work at raising our grandchildren. It's exhausting to watch, and when I look back on the first years of motherhood for my bride, I carry many regrets and wishes for do overs.

I wish there would have been a tool like "Live Happily Ever After" because I would have scored very low, and it would have woken me up to my lack of time being spent with both my bride and my little son. This was never my intention, but that's why taking an evaluation is so important. It reveals things to you that you otherwise wouldn't have knowledge of. Clearly had I been more aware, I would have taken longer to finish college and spent more time with Lynne and my son. I loved them very much, but you would never have seen that from my calendar. If you can't see it from looking at your calendar, changes need to be made.

The only excuse I have is ignorance. Lynne was always kind and affectionate to me. She cared for almost all of the household responsibilities, and though I was appreciative, I failed to ever ask if my choices caused her to be lonely. Loneliness is one of the most painful emotions. Many couples live together without the awareness that their partner is lonely. Loneliness puts a relationship at great risk. I never intended to do that, but intentions don't solve the problem of creating an environment of loneliness.

Lynne never accused me of not being a good husband. She has always spoken very kind words when she speaks about our marriage, but I know I could have done much better. I just didn't know. We got married young because I couldn't stand to be away from her. To this day when she is gone, even if I have children and grandchildren around me, I miss her.

Not long ago she was doing some business consulting for a wonderful resort in Blowing Rock, North Carolina. The resort is called Chetola (www.Chetola.com) and it feels like our second home. If you need a tune up on your marriage make reservations there and ask to stay in one of the "secret rooms." These rooms are very private and often politicians or celebrities stay in these 8 rooms at the "Inn." Each room has a fireplace, large bathtub and privacy. You can have breakfast in bed, there is a private library with a wine and cheese party every evening for the guests, warm chocolate chip cookies for an evening snack. Yum! Use this time to get to know each other, take walks around a lake connected to the property and invest in your relationship.

Getting back to my wife being gone doing consulting at Chetola Resort for two weeks, after five days I missed her so much that I bought airline tickets and told her I was coming to see her. I was now behaving the way I should have during our first couple of years of marriage. She welcomed me gladly and the owners were so glad I came. Even after all the years of marriage, there is no person I would rather spend time with, even if it means waiting until she is done working.

In the Bible is describes marriage as the two becoming one. This merging is not automatic. It's not because you signed a marriage license. It is a result of spending as much time as possible together, sharing your heart and body and making love an action verb.

In the subcategories to follow you will see the components that "Live Happily Ever After" measures to score your broad category of Companionship. If you discover that life was hectic like mine in the early days of marriage, and you didn't score as well as you hoped to, then it's time to make major changes. My desire is the advice that I share from my own failing will be helpful to you.

Time

There are many things that humans can create more of, however time is not one of them. We are born and one day we will die. Even if we are blessed to find that special person we want to share our lives with, we are never guaranteed a certain number of years.

Most of us take time for granted, and we get busy and believe that there will always be tomorrow to work on our important relationships. Sadly, that is not true. It's not just quality time, but also quantity of time that builds a strong relationship. When a couple gets married, they aren't just adding a person to their lives. If they want to be successful in their relationship, they have to completely reprioritize their lives.

In the Old Testament there is some valuable teaching, and also a great example, that I wish our culture could adopt in some way. We are told that if a man was getting married, even if Israel was at war, he was to take a year off of his career, to focus on learning to make his wife happy. WOW! I don't think that any such law exists today, but can you imagine how strong relationships would be if you could take a year away and just be together? Guys, notice that it was men that had to learn how to make our wives happy. There is no mention of wives needing to learn that lesson.

I defied this teaching big time when we first got married. As I shared above, I worked full-time and went to school full-time. What I was ashamed to mention previously, is that I graduated in three years. How crazy was I? I had all of the excuses down, I saved a lot of money, I could get on with graduate school sooner … I was a fool. I was totally unaware of the toll it was taking on my wife. I wish I could have taken

"Live Happily Ever After" and seen my score. I guarantee it was far below my grade point average.

I know there are seasons in life where we don't have full control of our choice to spend more time together. I think of the heroes that serve in our military for example, who often, along with their spouse, sacrifice so much for us. But when we do have control, it is necessary to give our beloved priority of our time.

When I was in high school, my plan was to become a physician. I am so glad that I changed my career path. I have many friends who are wonderful physicians. Years ago, my personal physician would spend an hour every year doing an extremely thorough physical on me and watched over my health. The truth was, he was such a devoted physician, that he failed as a husband. If he had offered her one hour a day with the intensity of attention that he gave me, he wouldn't have gotten a divorce. There are many fields that require an abundance of our time, and I often ask why?

Anyone who is in the car sales business works 50-60 hours a week. In the state I live in, you can't sell cars on Sunday's, otherwise I think the number of hours would be even higher. I have had many friends who have been very successful in this industry, but you can't invent more hours in a day. I think it would be better to give up a sale to another staff member and spend more time at home.

I already mentioned how painful loneliness is. Loneliness puts your marriage at risk. If your spouse is lonely, there are plenty of other lonely people that will steal away the one you promised to give your highest priority to. The word priority is interesting. It is a word that creates a value system. It forces you to say "no" to something because something else is more important. When we made a commitment to our partner, it was about making them the most important priority in our life, next to God.

Then reality hits and you have to pay the bills, and your boss asks you just once to stay late to finish a project. Then children come along with even more bills, and there is so much going on in your life that you don't think about priorities. Once you begin this cycle, a pattern begins to change your "lived out" priorities. You might recite the proper order, but your schedule gives you away.

One day when my children were about 6 and 8 years old, they had an argument. They came running to me and asked who I loved more. I said, "That's easy. I love your Mom more." Somehow this all made sense to them. For a stable household to exist, our children need to hear those priorities and see them lived out.

I have learned that I have to say "no" to some things in order to say "yes" to the best thing. I have often said "no" to someone, come home early and my wife asked, "Why are you home?" I told her that I was practicing saying "no" to others, so I could say "yes" to her. Those made for some of our most special moments and memories.

I know that there will always be emergencies that will throw us off, but if you aren't spending both "quality" and "quantity" time with your spouse, you are putting your relationship in danger.

It's so easy to let our lives get out of control. Lynne and I kept separate calendars for many years. We would do weekly updates to make sure we got the kids to the right places at the right time. We thought we were managing our time wisely and there was still enough "us" time. Slowly, as I assumed more responsibilities, my calendar would fill up sooner, often months ahead. I was traveling much more and when we finally got to overlapping our calendars, every day and night was taken. It happened so gradually that we just thought the next month was going to be better, but as we flipped pages to the next month, it was even worse.

We were reaching a point where we were almost living separate lives. Lynne was a school teacher and took her job very seriously. She always arrived an hour early and stayed late correcting papers or planning for the next week.

I was a pastor of a church that we had started and was now nearing 1,000 in attendance each week. I'm not overly gifted in any area except truly loving people and believing the difference that Jesus

Christ can make in their lives. This meant it took me longer to study for my sermon each week. I wanted my message to be Biblically accurate and relevant with clear applications. I was blessed to have hired a great staff, but that required a lot of meetings. Churches have lots of evening meetings that either Lynne or I would attend. Lynne was an unpaid worship pastor for 15 of the 20 years we served that church. She has amazing music skills and led a worship team which met for about 2 ½ hours on Wednesday nights. Then there were all of these wonderful people who came each week and would want to meet with me about getting married, questions about their faith or the problems they were facing. In addition, I was being asked to travel a couple of days each week which I loved, because I could invest in younger leaders and watch them grow.

One day Lynne and I sat down and we agreed that something needed to change. We were trapped into a world of our own creation. Everything we spent time on was "good" and "important." What could we do?

You may not have the same activities on your calendar that we had, but every couple reaches a point between work, kids, and all the household responsibilities separate you the way they did us. No time for each other. Lynne made one of the hardest and most sacrificial choices she could ever make. She decided to inquire about the possibility of doing a job share with another teacher the following year. To fully understand how big a decision this was, you'd have to understand Lynne's love for her students. This was no small sacrifice. It turned out that Lynne taught 3 days per week and the other teacher taught 2 days per week. She loved teaching, but she loved me more.

I also talked with the leadership of the church about our busy schedule, and they were very helpful in hiring more staff and narrowing down my responsibilities. I still traveled, but Lynne would often come with me, and most of the time the insights she shared with people were the most appreciated. We began to get control of our schedule and were spending far more time together. It made a huge positive impact on our relationship.

We intentionally had to work hard at saying "no" to others in order to say "yes" to each other. Lynne is the hero of this story. She found a way of finding a solution that allowed us to get our schedule under control. This was a far more critical time in our lives than we fully understood. After 20 years of serving this amazing church, we were about to be asked to take a leadership position that required us to move to Orlando, Florida. We felt lead to accept the position. It was one of the hardest choices we ever made. Leaving a church we started and the people we loved most was heartrending.

The good thing for our relationship was that it gave us an opportunity to create a common calendar where our highest priority was to spend time with each other. Our jobs were different, but we worked at the same organization, so we saw each other often. Making each other a priority was difficult, but very worth it in the long run. You can't invent time. We were both busy doing good things ... too busy. We had to take a radical step, lead by Lynne, and then together moving and establishing boundaries to protect our us time.

I have learned through the years that without intending to, I will always disappoint someone. I learned the hard way, to never become so overcommitted that I would disappoint my bride. Please learn from my mistake. Doing good doesn't mean you are doing the best. When you defined your relationship as "committed," that doesn't mean to give merely leftover time to your lover.

The moral of this story is I found myself trapped. I didn't want to disappoint anyone and by doing so, I was disappointing everyone. Priorities are best evidenced when there is a shortage of them. For us it was a shortage of time. We decided that our relationship was important enough to make some drastic changes. Our relationship then could have been described as "functional" and "productive," rather than passionate. Are you spending enough time together to grow your relationship? Please learn from our story and make whatever changes are necessary to spend enough time together.

I do want to mention that there are certain jobs that are seasonal. These careers have seasons of extreme work, like accountants during tax season, or retail around the Christmas season. If you are married to someone in one of those careers, realize that this will be a cycle in your year and do everything in your power to make sure to accommodate them. Do more of the housework, take more responsibilities with the children, or hire help if you need to. Do whatever is necessary so your time together will be high quality. The advice I am giving has to be contextualized through your lives, but time is essential to building an intimate relationship. Please practice saying "no" in order to say "yes" to the love of your life. It may take some creativity, or some difficult changes, but you can arrange to spend enough time together if you put your mind to it. If not, then take a different job or live more simply. I promise you will live a much more fulfilling life. At the end of your life, you will never regret spending too much time with the one you love most. After all, your job or your hobbies won't be sitting next to your deathbed; but hopefully your spouse will be.

Helpful Hints:

• Companionship is one of the great benefits of relationship. If you truly want to have a successful relationship, you must establish new priorities after you decide that this is a committed relationship. This should show your partner that he or she is the most important. One key to being successful is learning to say "no" to opportunities or relationships in order to say "yes" to your partner. Get in the habit early of saying "no" in order to spend time with your beloved.

• Do your best to go to bed at the same time. Even if you have had a pattern previously of staying up late or going to bed very early, discuss a time that will work for both of you and enjoy the end of every day in each other's arms.

• Be careful not to treat social media, emails, texts or phone calls as a higher priority than your partner. During a meal, put away your phone, turn off the television and develop a healthy pattern of listening and sharing with your partner.

• Think about how much fun you had together when you were dating. Do some of the same things now or come up with some new ideas that you both would enjoy.

Activities

Most of our lives have structures built in. My wife was a school teacher for 15 years where there was no flexibility. At the beginning of each school year, we would take our calendar and mark off every holiday or day off she had during the school year. I built my calendar around those dates, and they became sacred to our family.

There are always basic structures that our jobs, kids and holidays bring. Your task is to plan ahead and use vacation days to capture opportunities for building shared family memories. If you don't plan ahead, you will always be saying, "We should have" rather than "We did"

There are many different types of activities that you can be involved in. Because this isn't a book on parenting, I want to stay focused on your relationship with the most important person in your life. Think for a moment about your favorite things to do. It probably didn't take long to come up with a list. Now, think about your partner's favorite things. Can you list any? Do you do anything together? When I asked that question to people who came to see me as a pastor, most had a difficult time coming up with a list. I would ask the husband, write down what he'd say, and then invite their spouse to come back in the room. It turned out that most couples were unable to get even one answer correct. I hope this is a wake-up call. How capable are you of sharing the favorite activities of the person you should know best?

Years ago, I read a book, and I wish I could remember its name. The book was about the use of leisure time. In the book the author said that leisure time is often confused with "lazy time." The author went on to state that it is during this time that we invest in the most important parts of our lives. It is in these hours that we build love relationships, work on physical fitness, grow in our faith, spend time with our children and family. There is not enough leisure time to go around. We have to plan ahead to capture memories.

As for your spouse, it's great to become their best friend. Friendships are often built on shared activities. I shared earlier how Lynne and I were even actively engaged in each other's careers. We also made decisions each year to jointly learn about a different subject. It was easy to talk because we were constantly learning about a new area of interest. One of our together activities was working on fitness together, and it was fun to watch each other get stronger. This has been a lifelong pursuit which is not only healthy but also allows us to spend time together.

Each couple can determine what activities they want to try. There was a church bowling league that got started, and one year we decided to join. We spent more time laughing than bowling. I learned how uncoordinated I was. I also learned how much fun it was to get a strike. We lead Bible studies together, took up biking, and a host of other activities that stretched us and were fun.

We read the same books, both fiction and non-fiction, and again it was easy to talk because we had chosen to overlap our lives with activities. It's too easy for relationships to become utilitarian where living together "works" to pay the bills, take care the kids, cook and clean. All those things need to be taken care of so that you can share time growing together through activities.

I would encourage you to be open minded. Try new things together. If you don't enjoy them, you can move on to something else. A recent activity for us has been to get involved in a local arboretum and art museum, located in an old mansion in the city in which we live. They always have traveling art from very skilled artists and a beautiful garden to walk through. If we end up with some extra time, even an hour or so, we walk over to this beautiful facility and just talk.

We have grandchildren that we adore and treasure the time that we get to welcome them into our house. We each try to enrich their lives in different ways. I have learned that being a grandmother trumps everything. I can find myself sitting on the couch alone with a 2-year-old and a 4-year-old piled on grandma's lap. What a beautiful picture of the life we have shared.

There are endless ideas that you can engage in. We have friends who love dinner and wine tasting. Others who like to travel, and some who enjoy going to movies or finding their favorite television series.

I love Lynne. I also really like Lynne. She is smart and talented, she loves to laugh ... usually at my expense. She is kind and loving and adventurous. As long as the two of us are together, there is always a way to enjoy activities.

Our latest adventure is to learn how to play chess. We bought the chess board and want to learn strategy, and not just thinking one move ahead. There are hundreds of activities that allow our lives to overlap. It's where they overlap that we have opportunity to grow our relationship.

We still maintain great friendships individually. Our lives are full with our family and friends, but we have been careful to overlap our lives with activities that allow us to enjoy each other and build memories.

Helpful Hints:

• Activities are not only good for your health, but shared activities are very good for your relationship. Having fun together helps to create an environment where as a couple, you become best friends. If your partner has interests in an area, choose to join them and enjoy their passions. You will discover that most of the time you enjoy the activity too, if you see it from their perspective.

• Develop a bucket list of activities you'd like to experience with your partner and have fun setting a time frame and sequence to check them off.

• Activities or hobbies can either draw you close or push you apart. Your relationship is more important than any activity you would choose to do separately. There is nothing wrong with spending some time alone but be careful that your passions never steal away your passion for your partner.

Adventures

Activity fits within the structure of your combined calendars. Adventures are memory builders that interrupt your calendar and usually involve new experiences. Adventures cause us to break out of any rut we may have accidently gotten into.

When we were newly married and extremely poor, it may have been a camping trip or a stay at a timeshare. We would decide where we wanted to go and arrange months ahead and then the week before Lynne would "pre-nest." She is the most organized person ever. I remember a timeshare that we often went to had designated drawers for treats which our children rarely had and looked forward to. Every time we went to this "home away from home" the normal rules were forgotten. In the Bible it would be called the year of Jubilee. Bedtimes were extended, treats were available, family biking and swimming were adventures enjoyed and to this day, remembered. I once took out a small sailboat and the wind must have been blowing just right. I felt like a pro and invited my family to come aboard. Everything started out great. Our sail caught wind, and we quickly sailed a long way from the resort. The part that I couldn't quite figure out was how to get back against the wind. I was so thankful, and humbled, when a kind boater offered to bring us back. I can't tell you how many times we've relived that story. It was an adventure that didn't end up quite the way I expected but it became a memory worth reminiscing about.

While pastoring a church in Oshkosh, Wisconsin, I had opportunities to mentor pastors in other areas of the country. I hated leaving home, but I also had a great time building new friendships. One of the huge benefits was the frequent flyer miles that were available to create adventures for my wife and me, and often for our entire family. I remember our first family trip by air. We went with my older brother's family to a meeting in California. We were all so excited, and our children had a great time. On the way home, the flight was cancelled, and the airline put us up at the Hilton Hotel at LAX, which was way out of our price range, complete with food vouchers. We couldn't even spend all the food money. What a wonderful memory!

When my wife started teaching school, we wanted our children to experience more of the country. With my frequent flyer miles, we went to Washington D.C. and even Hawaii. It took careful planning and saving money, but we were always talking about the next adventure we could have together.

In addition to our family trips, Lynne and I would engage in big and small adventures. It doesn't have to be expensive; it just has to be special. It's really all about being together and experiencing new things. A picnic while exploring your city can be great fun. ALWAYS have an adventure on the calendar. By prioritizing these times, we have seen more of the world than we could have ever imagined. We can always say, "Remember when …" Adventures build memories that can never be taken away.

Here's a suggestion. Go onto the internet and search for "local adventures" or "adventures within 300 miles." I'm sure that there are exciting things to see close to home. Also begin a "bucket list" of adventures that you are willing to plan five years out. You will have time to save money for it, and you will have a fun and interesting time discovering information that will help you plan the memory.

"Live Happily Ever After" is a tool to measure how you are doing in "Companionship" that help us achieve the closeness that comes from being together. This is such a fun area to develop in your relationship. The possibilities are endless. Try to be open minded about new ideas. A true adventure often takes you outside of your comfort zone and with it, builds a lifelong memory.

Chapter 3:
CONFIDANT

One of the most important aspects of a committed relationship is the ability to share everything and anything with your spouse, without fear of being judged or having it thrown back in your face during a challenging time. Building this level of intimacy is challenging. Yet, it such a beautiful picture of intimacy within your relationship to fully know and be fully known. The greatest way to destroy trust is for you to ever tell another person any of these conversations shared in confidence.

I was raised in a home where my parents would have been better off divorced. There were many secrets in my life when I met Lynne. I can remember sharing with her little things at first about my growing up experiences. When she responded with compassion, I could tell that she would never tell anyone what I had shared with her. This level was a test to see if I could trust her.

I hope you grew up in the perfect home, but there is likely a top ten list of secrets that you don't want anyone to know. Because Lynne responded in such a sensitive way, I opened up more and more. She responded in the same loving way, often weeping over hurts that I had experienced and always affirming her love for me. I knew right then that I loved her. I had shared the worst memories and the most vulnerable things in my life, and she didn't judge me, but only loved me more.

Even during our early years of marriage, I would uncover something from my past that was hidden deep inside. I would share it with her without any hesitancy, because over the years, she had been consistently kind and understanding. My past did not change her vision of my future.

Lynne's past wasn't anything like mine, but there were things that she, too, had never shared with anyone. I responded with the same grace that she had poured over me. This aspect of our relationship quelled any questions about our future together. We were a safe haven for each other.

All of us have a backstory. By sharing our past with someone we love, we should sever the hurt and no longer have to carry it with us. In committed relationships, you become each other's confidant. A confidant accepts you, and all the experiences that have shaped you, without judgement and always in love.

This is the next broad area that "Live Happily Ever After" measures. If you have broken a trust, you can gain it back, but it may take a long time of being absolutely faithful. Be very careful not to break that trust again. Don't share personal information that has been given to you in confidence. This is one of the defining points in building intimacy into your relationship.

Trust

I was a Boy Scout growing up. The first attribute that you pledge is to be is trustworthy. It is an all-encompassing word about your integrity. A relationship without trust cannot grow. I have always been an advocate for telling the truth. I would rather have a person reject me for who I really am, rather than be a friend based on a lie.

When Lynne and I began dating she was easy to talk to. For me some of the subjects that had shaped my life weren't easy to talk about. The more I knew her, the more I feared her discovering the real me and not being interested in me. Previously I shared that Lynne became a safe place for me, and eventually she learned things about me that no one else in the world knew. My hopes, dreams, and fears poured out into this young woman whom I trusted more than anyone else.

Eventually I didn't bother with the good stuff. I went right to my deepest hurts and the baggage I carried. Her love for me was stronger than my past. We have been married for over 42 years now, and never once has she betrayed my trust. Quite the opposite. She showed me how my past contributed to the man I could become. She believed in me. She knew everything there was to know and yet loved me. How amazing. I have done my very best to never abuse that trust. I can't think of a lie I've told her, unless it was a surprise party for her. After being accepted for the man I could become, I was highly motivated to become that man.

Trust is an amazing gift, especially if you have been hurt by others. I would venture to say that all of us have had a trust broken in one way or another. This makes reaching a place of total trust very difficult. Trust should be a progressive goal. At first you establish a goal to see if a person is honest with you and dependable. My father would promise my mother he would be home for dinner with the family but would rarely show up. I would wake up in the morning only to see a plate of uneaten food still on the table. Talk is cheap, and the standards that I'm talking about are far higher than telling someone something that you think they want to hear. It is living out the words that you speak.

When a couple reaches a level of trust in their relationship, they tend to let down their guard. It is then that they can be taken advantage of by a partner that doesn't have integrity. There are certain absolutes that no one should ever have to experience once they have been told that they are loved by another. Long before "I love you" should be spoken, it should be understood by both parties that saying those words means absolute honesty, fidelity and no manipulation of what is true. This is what love means. Love is lived out with a greater commitment to the other, than yourself.

Sadly, I have had too many people share with me, through tears that their spouse had cheated on them. How does a person recover from that? I would meet with the offender, and they would explain that, "It just happened, and it will never happen again." Sadly, the best predictor of future behavior is past behavior.

By the way, nothing "just happens." Many people are oblivious to the fact that someone is threatening their relationship. There are likely people targeting you or your spouse right now who will slowly work their way into your lives. Unless you are proactive and alert, very poor, irredeemable decisions can be made.

It doesn't just happen. Situations were occurring previous to the mistake. It feels good to be flattered. A joke here, a touch there. Soon, which once seemed off limits now seems acceptable. I am a firm believer in creating boundaries within my life so that there is little to no possibility for anything like that to happen. I mentioned that I traveled weekly for many years. Often they were lonely trips. I would sit next to business travelers who would tell me stories of an accidental affair, a hook up, or a one-night stand. They didn't seem to have a strong moral compass to begin with, so when the opportunity arose, they took it.

Prior to ever leaving on a trip, I reminded myself what I had to lose if I ever made a poor decision such as that. By investing deeply in our marriage, I never wanted to put our relationship at risk. I shared with Lynne a number of choices that I made to create a boundary around my life, so that both of us would feel secure. The most basic decision I made was calling her several times a day to update her on my trip and remind her of my love for her.

If you are in a business that requires frequent travel, make choices prior to ever having a temptation approach you. I've known many pilots who have talked to me about what it's like to live that lifestyle. All of them were great men, but they told me how often infidelity takes place. Each of them shared with me the ways they kept themselves accountable in their marriage relationship. Trust is usually tested, but when proved faithful, grows stronger.

If you have been cheated on, and many of you reading this have been, I am sincerely sorry for the hurt that you have felt. I want to assure you that not everyone is like that. Try to think about what you would require to feel safe in a relationship. If you begin to date again, go slowly. If someone goes out of your boundaries, end the relationship quickly. You don't want to be taken advantage of and hurt again.

Lastly, I want to share with you that there is a great correlation between substance abuse and infidelity. My father struggled greatly with alcohol. Often he found himself in environments where cheating was prevalent. The effects of alcohol and other substances, open people up to making poor decisions. This is not an environment to find a forever relationship. If you find yourself in this situation, please be aware that alcohol or drugs can become more important than a relationship. Choose wisely, who you will spend time with and who you will give your heart to.

If you are an addict, please get help. This might just be the motivation you need to change your life. People who are addicts always choose what they are addicted to over anything or anyone else. I know all too well the pain of addiction. My father died at just 46-years-old from alcoholism, and our oldest son lost his life to drug addiction at the young age of 27.

If you are married to an addict, I understand your pain. First, they made a poor decision to use. It doesn't take long for the alcohol or drugs to be in control of their thoughts, body and entire life. It will not get better on its own. I don't want you to share the devasting hurts that I have in my life. Please reach out to a professional that can help guide you in the best choice for your life.

When you come into a committed relationship, an absolute key is taking off the masks that are so easy to wear, and reveal who you are, warts and all. This is the real you. If you are truly going to have an intimate relationship, you want to know and be known. Secrets come out at the most inopportune times, and usually cause some damage to your relationship. Trust is not a destination, but a constant journey of revealing more and more about who you are. Even now into my 60's, I'm still discovering new things about myself. I expect through the rest of my life there will be new discoveries about who I am and who I'm growing to be. You don't reach trust and stay there. Trust must continue to grow. There is great freedom when you don't have anything to hide or prove. I have been blessed to be accepted for all that I am and all that I'm not. I don't have to pretend.

I believe that Lynne feels exactly the same way. I want her to have the confidence that I love her more than anything she's experienced in her past or carries into the present. I don't want her to ever feel she needs to hide anything from me.

After living this way consistently from dating, to engagement, to marriage and now 42 years later, I can say this is how it's supposed to be. The world can reject me, but I will be just fine as long as Lynne's arms are open wide.

Helpful Hints:

- Do an inventory of conversations that you have with friends. Are there private matters that your partner would not want you to share that you have shared in the past?
- Come to an understanding about what is private between the two of you and don't break that trust. If you do, then your partner is going to think hard about whether or not they can share with you all of the aspects of their life.
- Be honest with your partner if they ask you a question. Even if they are upset with your answer, the truth is still the best way to proceed.

• Don't pretend to be someone that you aren't. Love isn't based upon exaggerated statements about who you are or what you've done.

Vulnerability

We never exploit someone's vulnerabilities.

When Lynne and I were first dating, a group of friends invited us out to go roller skating at an indoor roller rink. We were at the stage of our relationship that it was difficult to say "no" to any suggestion. I wasn't a skilled skater, but I could go around in circles. I was looking forward to this experience, because it was a good opportunity to hold her hand as we were skating. Let me preface this and say some of you are not going to like me after reading this story.

What I didn't realize was that Lynne had never skated before. She grew up near a small town that didn't have a skating rink, and I made the foolish assumption that if I could do something, anyone could do it. She laced up her skates and stood up. She looked like a pro. I took her hand, and we made our way out onto the rink. She held my right hand, and I guess I overestimated her abilities as we skated faster. She certainly had a tight grip on my hand, and she seemed like she was doing perfectly well until we both fell down right in the middle of the rink. I can still hear the whistle blowing after all these years, alerting others to fallen bodies on the rink. I got up quickly and started skating again to prevent other skaters from tripping over us, fully expecting Lynne to be right behind me. Skating around the circle, I heard the whistle keep blowing and then saw my date ... this girl that I was really fond of, crawling across to the edge of the rink, with tears in her eyes. She couldn't get up and she felt totally embarrassed, especially around my friends that she didn't know. Her only concern was getting as far away from everyone as possible. After I saw her distress, I felt so badly that I hadn't helped her get up. She crawled to a chair, and to this day, has never put on another pair of roller skates. Lynne told me she couldn't skate, but I didn't believe her. I put my shy, beautiful, and hopefully still girlfriend, in a place of great vulnerability. Just thinking about it right now makes me feel awful.

The rest of the night wasn't my favorite time to be with her. I felt like a jerk and a large number of girls at the roller rink let me know that they agreed. I learned an important lesson. I never again wanted to put Lynne into a vulnerable position where she experienced fear or embarrassment if I had any control over the situation. To the best of my knowledge, I learned my lesson.

Vulnerability isn't something you can demand. It is one of the greatest gifts a person can give to another. It is based upon a very high level of trust. If someone makes themselves vulnerable to you, treat it as a treasure. It is something that can be easily lost and never recovered.

I am so thankful that our relationship continued and grew to the place that, after permission from her father, I got down on one knee, looked into her eyes and asked her to marry me. She said yes! It is one of the happiest days of my life. I put a ring on her finger that cost $207. I had never spent that much money before, and she looked at it like it was worth a million dollars.

We planned the wedding, and after getting married, went on our honeymoon. It consisted of three nights staying at a Motel 6 that had an inch gap at the bottom of the door. The toilet ran all night. We froze all night, because the heat didn't work correctly and it was a true 30 degrees below zero during that January, Midwest winter. I didn't realize how poor we were. I was thrilled to have this lovely woman as my bride, lying beside me. She made me feel grown up, and we started our married life.

It was common to get married young in the seventies. I was only 21, but I felt very mature. My true maturity level, however, was not where Lynne would have liked it to be. Growing up with four siblings, we often would sneak up behind one of them and say "Boo!" just to watch their reaction. Each of us gave as much as we received. We also would walk up and tickle each other.

With all that said, for no good reason, I somehow transferred my bad sibling behavior into my early days of marriage. I would walk up behind Lynne and tickle her ... not for very long, but enough to bring her discomfort and show my immaturity. One day I walked up to her and reached out my arms to hug her, and I saw her react by putting her arms very close to her body in a position to protect herself from being tickled. My touch had become a negative response, not a loving embrace. I quickly came to my senses after seeing the look on her face. At that moment, I decided that my hands would never again be used for anything other than protecting her. I didn't tell her my decision, but in the last 41 years I have never touched her except to show her my love. I waited to see how long it would take for me to approach her and she wouldn't respond in a defensive posture, and it was about five years. Many years later, I told her the decision I had made. I wanted her to be able to fully expose herself to me in total vulnerability. I am so grateful that I gained that insight.

Over the decades I have done my very best to treasure her every day. Her gift back to me was vulnerability that she has never taken back. I am a blessed man.

Helpful Hints:

- Show respect to your partner when they share something with you that was difficult to reveal. Thank them and let them know it was very meaningful that they shared what they did.
- NEVER laugh or tease when your partner shares something meaningful or private with you.
- Understand that it is the greatest honor that anyone would ever allow themselves to be vulnerable with you.
- Re-evaluate your touch. Does your partner ever protect themselves from your silly antics that you think is funny?
- Take the time to periodically share with each other the new ways you are growing and changing.

Friendship

I mentioned earlier, that the word "friend" has drastically changed because of social media. Through the years I was around many people as the church I pastored became very large. I loved them. I wanted to care for the needs of each of them, which was impossible. I actually felt greater satisfaction when the church was small enough that true friendships were forged and maintained. I am blessed to have some men who are true friends. I know that they would do anything they could to help me. They speak truth into my life. I am so thankful for each of them.

I always saw Lynne as my "best friend." She meant everything to me. One day we were talking about friendships, and she told me she was looking for a "best friend." That was another one of the days that my life changed. She saw me as many wonderful things, but probably wouldn't have put "friend" on the list.

After hearing her say that she wanted a "best friend," I reviewed our relationship. I started to really think of the traits of a friend and then privately tried to make them a part of our relationship. It is very healthy for people to have friends other than their spouse, but I have come to believe that it is essential that you are very good friends with your spouse. I learned from my past mistakes that talk is cheap, so I never told her the changes that I was making. It didn't talk long, and I saw a major change in our relationship because I began treating her like I wanted her to be my best friend.

Traits of true friendship from lifehack.org

    1. A great listener.

    2. Always has your back.

    3. Accepts you at your worst.

    4. Loves you.

    5. Can talk about personal things.

    6. Knows how to make you smile.

    7. Gives honest opinions.

    8. Sticks by your side.

    9. Encourages you.

    10. Is dependable.

    11. Isn't judgmental.

    12. Celebrates your success.

From the list above, you can see that it takes clear intention and perseverance over time to become close friends. I'm far from perfect, but my efforts have certainly paid off. Lynne is definitely my best friend, and just before writing these words I asked Lynne who her best friend was. Thankfully she said, "You are!" This isn't just about Lynne's and my relationship, but your relationship, too. If you want to reach the place of being your partner's confidant, it requires trust, vulnerability and friendship.

Helpful Hints:

- Remember that friendship is a solemn partnership with another person where you take each other's side and believe, that together, you can conquer any challenge. Any corrections are saved for another time or discussion.

- Plan a surprise date for your partner that includes things they would love to do.

- Learn the interests of your partner. Ask questions and be involved.

- Everyone needs fun. Dates don't have to be expensive, so spend some time brainstorming. Even an hour alone can spice up a relationship.
- Do something that your partner would enjoy doing with other friends. Let them know you are interested in their desires, even if it may be out of your comfort zone or out of the ordinary for you.

Chapter 4:
CONSUMMATE

Growing closer together should be the ultimate goal for any couple. You want to knit your lives so closely together, that it would be very difficult to unravel your relationship. As we have followed the assessment "Live Happily Ever After," we have discussed some very important broad topics of Communication, Companionship and Confidence. Putting effort into these areas will grow your relationship beyond what you can imagine. If you ignore them, you are likely to become another statistic of an unhappy marriage.

We now move on to the fourth major topic, which I consider the place where all of your hard work intersects, and you are personally benefited from the attention that you have previously invested in your relationship. The broad category is Consummate. By definition, the word means "to complete." It can be used to describe the completion of a business deal, the sale of a house, or in a relationship it means becoming physically intimate.

I have always been a person who isn't quite happy until a project of mine is completely finished. Lynne and I have bought homes on a low budget that became beautiful homes with a lot of love and hard work. Once I got started on a project, I couldn't stop until the last detail was done. Some people enjoy the process; with me it's all about the finished product, and then having Lynne work her magic on it. That's when I can relax and truly enjoy the accomplishment.

This is why the prior categories of Communication, Companionship and Confidence are so essential. If you are remodeling a house, you have to do things in a certain order. You must do the electrical and plumbing before you put up the sheet rock. If you do the sheet rock first, your wall might look complete, but it will only be a mirage, because the essential work was never completed.

If you truly want to consummate your committed relationship, you must build things in the proper order. If you don't, then you are cheating yourself from experiencing what your relationship could be like, and you will be disappointed.

Lynne and I worked very hard before we were married to prepare for the big day, but truthfully, we weren't prepared. No one took the time to tell us the information that we really needed to know. I'm writing this book because I'm treating you as if you were one of the couples who come to me all excited about getting married. I want to share with you the truth about how to prepare marriage and what to expect. I want you to be prepared to "consummate" or complete your relationship. I don't want you to put sheet rock up before the electrical or plumbing. As you continue to read the subpoints of this chapter, I want you to constantly assess your relationship and ask yourself if you have worked diligently on the areas that preceded this chapter in the book. There is a reason why the assessment Live Happily Ever After was written in this order. I want all of the utilities finished before you get dressed up for the big day.

The highest legal form of a relationship is marriage. It is a contract that isn't official until both parties sign it on the dotted line. I am a strong advocate of marriage. Couples who are living together never have the security that they would have, if they were legally married.

I know there are reasons why people postpone marriage or live together. Usually, they have seen the hurt that comes when a divorce takes place. The problem with not legally formalizing your relationship is that it is never as secure. People are overreacting to what they have seen in unsuccessful marriages, by avoiding the "piece of paper." What they fail to understand is there isn't a need for a failed marriage if people diligently follow the steps outlined in this book. A person is deeply hurt when a relationship breaks down whether you are married or not.

Consummating the relationship, or as the dictionary says, "completing it," makes a bold statement when you intend to do whatever it takes to help this relationship prosper. I understand the fear because all of us have been hurt by broken relationships. If you are reading this now, you are likely in a relationship that you hope will grow into completion. Don't let other people's failures cause you to lower the bar on what a committed relationship should be. In this book, you have an outline of what is involved in building a strong, healthy relationship. You may not have known that you have to be proactive in building your relationship prior to reading this. Great marriages don't just happen. They are a result of hard work. If you are going to do the work, you might as well "complete" it through a public declaration of the love you have one for another.

If you are living together right now and are not married, have you asked your partner if they want to formalize your relationship? Bring it up early in the day and ask if it would be meaningful to them. You may discover that this "completion" of your relationship will guide you into a more fulfilling relationship.

There are several subpoints that bring your relationship to completion. The consummation of your hopes and dreams, within a formal commitment, makes it possible for your relationship to last forever.

Sexual Intimacy

Today it is common to hook up with someone. If you are feeling lonely tonight, there are websites with photos of people who are also looking to join you for the evening. Nothing serious or committed...just sex.

During my lifetime, people have become far more open in talking about sex, but I'm not certain that behaviors have really changed that much. The average age a person loses their virginity hasn't changed a whole lot since the World War 2 generation. People never talked about it, but there were a lot of marriages where babies followed 7-8 months later. Take a look back on your family genealogy, and you might discover that great grandma and great grandpa were friskier than you thought. The big difference was if a couple found themselves in this situation, they got married. They never went through the steps this book has mentioned prior to consummating their relationship. Often their relationship only grew to be utilitarian -

raising children and paying the mortgage. They may have functioned, but without the passion that was desired.

Today a person feels the need to apologize if they are a virgin. I believe that sexual intimacy is a very important part of marriage. Learning your partner's body and what they respond to in the security of a committed relationship, is a wonderful benefit. In a perfect world, couples would meet, grow their relationship, get married and then explore the joys of sexual intimacy. The reason I say that would be ideal is because every person you have ever slept with impacts your emotions, as well as your body.

There are certain diseases that you increase the likelihood of getting based upon the number of people you have slept with. Safe sex isn't really safe. We can protect ourselves to some degree against certain venereal diseases, but not all. The other problem is when you sleep with someone, your body is actually coming in contact with everyone that person has ever slept with. A huge percentage of the population has STD's. All of this frightens me. In a perfect world we would have one partner for a lifetime, but we don't live in a perfect world, and this reveals itself often in our sexual history. Whatever your past may be, I would encourage you to reevaluate what your life choices will be going forward.

Here is reality. We don't live in a perfect world. Prior to reading this book, we've all made life choices that are unchangeable. The feeling of guilt is often associated with sex, and that is never positive. Guilt always causes a person to pull away from what they feel guilty about. If one of you feel guilty about previous sexual decisions, you are limiting your ability to be a good lover to your partner. If you have regrets or hurts from previous relationships, do yourself and your partner a favor, and speak to a professional. This will help immensely as you move ahead in intimacy. You can't undo your past, but you can work through it.

Sharing our body with another is to bring completion to your relationship. I believe sexual intimacy is best shared in the committed relationship of marriage. It should be a wonderful celebration of all the work and time you have put into growing your relationship. Many couples "hook up" and then try to grow their relationship. I am not being judgmental, but I believe the sequence in which you grow your relationship impacts its long-term potential. Often, there is less motivation to work hard at Communication, Companionship and becoming a Confidant, when a couple is enjoying the Consummation part of the relationship. But going back to the building illustration, you don't want to put up the sheet rock before doing the electrical and plumbing.

I have talked to hundreds of couples that are frustrated with their sexual relationship. Lynne and I were frustrated. Lynne grew up in a very legalistic background where the only reference about sex was negative. It took her a long time to feel fully free to express herself sexually. I am so grateful that she was able to move past the negative stigma and enjoy the benefits of this gift.

I have to be honest here as well. We were both virgins when we married. We actually moved up our wedding date by six months, because I wanted to honor the commitment I made to her. I had only a man's perspective on sex in our early days of marriage. For a man it's pretty basic. You touch and are touched, your body responds, and upon ejaculation, you have an organism. Then a man is pretty worthless, at least for a while.

I fully expected sexual fulfillment to be as easy for Lynne as it was for me. It was not. We would have a wonderful sexual encounter where both of us were physically satisfied, and I thought I had figured her out. I would try to please her exactly the same way the next time with no success at all. I remember asking her why touching her the same way didn't always work and she would say, "It moved!" Ladies, you probably understand what Lynne was saying.

When couples would come to me and discuss problem areas, often they would want to talk about this private subject. What I discovered is that many women are far more complicated than men. If you are one of those women, please try to help your husband. Don't be shy. Honestly, if you don't tell him what you want and need, he won't ever succeed in one of his biggest desires which is to please you.

Men have complained to me about wanting a greater amount of sex in their relationship. I have given some thought about why women don't want to engage more. I've come to the conclusion that I don't think men would want to have sex without an orgasm. Guys, are you sure that she is enjoying the thrill of an orgasm? As men, we have to take this into consideration. We have to make sure that our partner feels safe and desirable, and we need to pay careful attention to what pleases her. Affirm her as she grows at becoming a great lover. The safer you make her feel and the more you focus on her rather than yourself, the greater likelihood that this will be an area of strength and pleasure in your relationship.

I was helping a couple with their pre-marriage counseling. Lynne and I always tried to coach couples together on this subject. They are a wonderful couple we really enjoyed meeting with. Both of them had waited for marriage to become intimate. She brought up in our meetings, that all of her girlfriends who were married had no interest in sex and wished they never had to have it again. She was terrified that this could happen to them.

Our discussions on sex were very honest and forthright. Usually there was a lot of giggling and red faces, even with couples who had been married for some time. Most couples are shy about talking about this subject, especially with a pastor and wife. We would share words the couple had never said aloud to each other. It didn't take long for us to gain their trust and discuss sex in detail. We gave some great biology lessons as we discovered how little a man knows about a woman's anatomy and a woman about a man. To be a good lover, you need to become an expert on your partner's body and mind. I wish more couples had candid conversations like we had with the couples that we talked with. Working with Lynne made the couple very comfortable, and soon they were asking questions they never expected. We spoke out of our mistakes, fears and misconceptions, but with hope of what could be.

I had mentioned that three months after a couple is married, I would do a checkup on how they were doing. When we met with the couple that I mentioned previously, I casually asked, "What is the best part of being married?" and without hesitation, she responded "Sex!" Her greatest fear became one of the core strengths in their relationship. I believe this can be true with every couple. That's why I think the sequence of when you become sexual needs to be after you have grown a truly committed relationship. If you have already been intimate, ask yourself if you need to take a step back and work at building the other important areas of your relationship before being intimate again. Take the sheetrock off, and add the utilities, and then finish a well-constructed relationship.

Please consider the importance of sequence in your relationship. I've known many couples who were living together, that wanted to push the restart button. They moved out, began dating and really invested in the areas you've already read about. They chose to limit their physical relationship to hugging and kissing. They forgot how wonderful that part of a relationship was. There was a growing desire to be physically intimate, but they waited until they grew through the foundational principles we've discussed. They then got engaged and planned a honeymoon with great anticipation for their wedding night. The couples I'm thinking of escalated the level of the sexual satisfaction many times over, because of their ability to talk, their deepening friendship and the trust they had built.

Many of us have been with our spouse for a long period of time and we could use a few tips on how to bring sexual magic back into the relationship. This is a very important area that most couples struggle in. Before I share some advice with you on how to spice things up, let me share with you that the reality is that many people, mostly woman, have had a very bad sexual experience prior to meeting you. I believe the statistic is one out of three women are sexually molested. If you are reading this and you have been a victim of such an awful assault, I want you to know that I am so sorry that you ever had that experience. You may carry the heavy weight of shame or guilt. I wish I could take away your past, but I can only let you know that there is hope. You may have been too embarrassed to have ever told anyone. I would encourage you to meet with a trusted professional that you feel safe with to try to deal with this terrible memory.

Because in the past a person abused you does not mean that you can't once again build trust and grow to have a wonderful physical relationship. It does mean however, that it is even more important that you wait to become sexual with someone. Go through the entire process mentioned in this book. If your partner isn't willing to wait, then they aren't the right person for you. This can be one of the most beautiful experiences in your life, both giving and receiving physical touch and pleasure. God made your body to enjoy this passion, but first take steps toward healing. If your partner has become your confidant, then you will have shared your past hurt with them. Both men and women carry the scars of being molested. Trust will return if you follow the necessary steps. I would encourage you to go slowly in any relationship, as you are working through the hurts of your past. Rather than wondering if you are getting "better," you will see quantitative results that will show you are regaining trust taking the Live Happily Ever After manual.

Here is some advice on how to add excitement to your intimate relationship. You might wonder where I would find the information that might help you improve your sexual relationship. I bet you would never guess that it's in the Bible of all places. Yes, God created sex and wants it to be meaningful, exciting, fun and fulfilling. Humans are the only part of God's creation that I know of that have sex just for fun, and not just for procreation.

The advice I'm going to share comes from the book of Proverbs when Solomon warns men not to fall into the trap of the seductive woman. This is good advice on boundaries to create in your life if you want to prevent yourself from being tempted and falling prey to adultery, but you can also turn it around and see the tools of the seductress and use them within your marriage to keep your romantic life fulfilling.

1) Be intentional

Proverbs 7 gives us some good ideas for sexual intimacy within the context of marriage.

10 Then out came a woman to meet him, dressed like a prostitute and with crafty intent.

I don't want you to focus on the wardrobe mentioned in this verse, I want you to notice that this woman made sex a priority. I want to encourage you to make it your goal to have a very fulfilling sex life. The woman mentioned was intentional at creating victims. Use the same intentionality to build your marriage. Some people have been raised in environments where they were told sex was wrong. As I mentioned, my wife Lynne had never once heard anything positive about sex. It took her some time to get past that legalism that is filled with guilt before she could really enjoy sex as God had intended. Have fun, get creative, and aim to please your partner.

2) Be available

12 now in the street, now in the squares, at every corner she lurks.

Once again, we can learn from this woman of the night. She was very available. Make sure that you make your sexual relationship a priority. I always advise couples to go to sleep at the same time. If you aren't in bed together, there won't be any sparks flying. For some people they choose days of the week that they prepare for and can anticipate making love. Discuss frequency, the best times for you both and what you both enjoy. Especially in our busy schedules and with small children, intentionality is a must!

3) Be passionate

13 She took hold of him and kissed him

This woman was well aware of how to have her way with men. Most men really enjoy being pursued by their spouse and initiating lovemaking. Men, don't get so lost in the physical act that you forget to share words that express the love and attraction you have for your wife. A flame goes out when people stop putting wood on the fire in order to create some passionate heat. What did you do while you were dating to "court" each other? Women, you cannot be too passionate or too forward in your desire for your man. Let him know you want him. Let him know of your desire for him through words, sexy attire, and smoldering looks. Be playful! These little things mean the world to your husband and shows him you treasure him.

4) Be expressive

13 She took hold of him and kissed him and with a brazen face she said: 14 "I have fellowship offerings at home; today I fulfilled my vows. 15 So I came out to meet you; I looked for you and have found you!

When a couple goes to bed, sometimes they haven't made clear what they are hoping for. The woman mentioned in Proverbs was proactive and very clear. I've heard it said that great sex at night begins at breakfast. If you start your day by expressing your love to your spouse and use whatever means necessary in showing your goal for the evening, both of you will be ready. Write love letters to each other. Express words after an especially intimate evening. Share how your partner is the only one you desire and how fulfilled you were.

5) Be creative

16 I have covered my bed with colored linens from Egypt. 17 I have perfumed my bed with myrrh, aloes and cinnamon.

This woman knew that most couples fall into a routine and have boring sex. She planned a creative experience. She aroused multiple senses and made the evening a night to remember.

Lynne has surprised me many times, in many ways and in many locations, which I won't get specific about. I have known the pleasure and intimacy of lovemaking where Lynne made extra efforts to make the experience memorable. Yes, sometimes sex is utilitarian, but that shouldn't be the norm. Go out of your comfort zone. Be a little crazy! Create your own private memories. Years later you will look back with great fondness and excitement. You'll remember the effort and passion that you shared.

6) Be positive

18 Come, let's drink deep of love till morning; let's enjoy ourselves with love!

Sadly, there are many who have had a bad experience sexually or they see imperfections in themselves and don't feel confident. Please try to get past that. Talk to a professional and come to realize that you spouse finds you beautiful and desirable. Don't look at personal flaws. Affirm your attraction to your partner. Women especially are affected by their appearance, if they don't think they look "perfect." This attitude can definitely affect the frequency and fun of lovemaking.

Helpful Hints:

- Let your partner know how attractive they are to you.
- Go shopping and surprise your spouse with something that makes you feel sexy, or better yet, go shopping together and find something that makes you both feel great!

- Remember that attraction starts in the brain before the physical act.
- Be creative in times, places and positions.
- Remember the old adage, sex begins at breakfast. How you treat each other through the day, will impact what your evening is like. Make sure that your hopes and intentions are clear so your partner can prepare.

Emotionally Connected

This is another essential point under consummate. A physical act can just be a biological function unless you have worked hard at developing a healthy emotional life.

Feeling loved is more important than making love. This again is why I think many couples do things out of proper sequence and struggle in their relationship.

Woman are often far more in touch with their feelings. This is a huge benefit for any man. There are only four core areas of life; physical, intellectual, spiritual and emotional. Many men, including me struggled to get in touch with my emotions. It is like living without one of your senses. Most of us can imagine losing our sight or the ability to feel touch. Just as we have only five senses and don't want to lose any of them, we also are limited to four domains that our lives reside in.

People with dementia have lost full use of their intellect. This is one of most people's greatest fears as they age. Our emotions are a critical part of our life. There are actually tools that measure emotional intelligence (EQI). We function as if we are missing something when we repress our emotions.

Emotions can be expressed differently by each person and there is no "right" way. Some people are very teary and others more stoic, yet both may have well developed emotions. Just like you can't judge intelligence from the outside, you can't make a judgement about a person's emotional health by just looking at how they process emotions.

Emotional health is not determined by how easily you cry. Emotional health is about an awareness of the emotions that are around you and that you respect them. It is the ability to feel and not just think.

I took the tool called EQI and went through it with a coach. This coach helped me turn what appeared to be a black and white world into color. I am forever grateful. Recognizing the emotions expressed around me helps me to be empathic in caring for other people. I grew up in a home with severe problems. To survive in a climate like that, I turned off some of my emotions. It affected me greatly.

I wanted to be more aware of my emotions and being married to Lynne created a very safe place for me to tell my story and have her ask "feeling" questions. At first, I didn't know how I felt. I could always describe in detail what I thought. It was with Lynne's help and the awareness that I was crippled in one of the four ways a person engages their world, I became motivated to develop this aspect of my life. I am sure that I need a lot of growth in each of the four areas listed. I am far more aware of emotions and how they allow me to give others insight into the world. It also allows me to feel the full range of emotions from grief to joy. From black and white television to HD full color television. You don't know what you are missing until you experience it.

A healthy emotional relationship is critical in building your relationship. If you don't quite understand emotions or have difficulty reading the emotions of others then follow the journey that I took and make that a priority.

Emotions aren't right or wrong, they are true to you. That is why you need to develop such intimacy with each other that you can protect and honor the emotions of your partner. People can argue facts, but emotions are defined by the person who is experiencing them. If you think that your emotions are overstated and that they aren't giving you an accurate view of your world, please see a professional counselor to help you. You may discover that you are perfectly fine, or you might discover you are depressed or struggle in some other way.

I found this definition of emotional health at familydoctor.org. "People who are emotionally healthy are in control of their thoughts, feelings, and behaviors. They are able to cope with life's challenges. They feel good about themselves and have good relationships. Being emotionally healthy does not mean you are happy all the time."

Helpful Hints:

- Take time to affirm your partner every day. Focus on their character and not just what they do for you or their appearance.
- If you feel that your conversations are not affirming to your partner or your relationship, stop and change the direction. Think about what is really important and ask yourself if this is a necessary and uplifting conversation.
- Make time to reminisce over highlights of your relationship. Talk about the fun and happy times or the times that were especially meaningful to you both.
- Be aware of times where your partner is exhausted or appears depressed and always be open to having them see a counselor or offering to go with them to see one.

Spiritually Bonded

I mentioned above that there are four realms we engage in. Emotionally, Physically, Intellectually and Spiritually. We need to grow in each of these areas as a couple if we are going to be truly successful.

In my teens I tried to be an atheist. I said I tried because the more I thought about it, the more absurd it became that creation was a random meaningless accident. I saw too much order in the universe that required a master designer. I also examined scientific laws and one of them is that something can't come from nothing. So, if there was a big bang that flung billions of galaxies into being, what preceded that. It took too much faith for me to be an atheist.

So, then I became an agnostic. An agnostic seemed like a pretty safe place to plant myself. Basically, agnostics believe that there is some force greater than we are who created all that we can see. However, a personal relationship with this force is not possible. This, of course, caused me problems when I started to think about morality and the sense that most people have of what is good. Why would love exist if an impersonal force created us. The more I tried to make that work, the more holes I saw in that belief system.

I then became aware that there must be a God. I wasn't sure what God was about, but I decided I would spend a season of my life trying to figure it out.

I examined religions that evaluated the orthodoxy of Buddhism, which elevated a man who never claimed to be a god, but a philosopher. I didn't want to commitment my life to someone who denied ever being god.

I then looked at the three major world religions; Christianity, Judaism and Islam. What I discovered is that they all believe in the God of Abraham. So, I picked up a Bible and read it. I agreed with the three world religions that believing in the God of Abraham brought everything into clarity. Each of those faiths have a different understanding of how to achieve a relationship with the God of Abraham.

The words of Jesus were overwhelming to me. I didn't earn a standing before God because of the things I do. God's love was expressed by Jesus's sacrifice on the cross. This made forgiveness through grace available to all mankind. Grace means that you didn't earn it. You can't earn it. All you have to do is open your heart and accept this relationship. I made that commitment when I was 17-years-old and the world has never looked the same since then. Things that didn't make sense before now were clear. I learned about the meaning of love and its roots in God Himself. God wanted me to resemble Him more by working on my life from the inside out. He wanted to be my teacher and leader. This was profound to me because I wasn't doing a very good job leading my own life.

I believe that people without this faith commitment are missing out on the greatest thing in the world. It fills your life with purpose and direction.

A shared faith or being Spiritually Bonded means that you are yielding to the same Teacher and Guide for your life. Couples who connect to this have a wonderful opportunity to understand life and their part in it from God's perspective.

Jesus is the most admired teacher of all time. His wisdom confounded those who thought they were wise. His humility became the greatest expression of love of all time.

When a couple follows Christ together, they grow closer together. They are led by the same Leader which means they have fewer disagreements with each other.

I did not set out to write a religious book but I can't exclude what I believe is a critical component to every marriage. So please don't ignore this subject. Coming in to a faith relationship with God has nothing to do with attending church, giving money, trying to be good, etc. It is recognizing God for who He is and accepting His forgiveness for all the things that we have done wrong. This is made possible by Jesus's sacrifice on the cross and His resurrection from the dead three days later.

This is the most important advice in the entire book. If you want a happy life and a successful committed relationship it begins here. It's a conversation with God, who is always listening. It's letting Him know that you believe in Jesus and you want to come into a personal relationship with Him. The great thing is God accepts everyone regardless of their past when we open our hearts up to Him.

Helpful Hints:

- Talk about what you are learning spiritually and ask your partner what he or she is learning.
- Visit churches to find one that you feel comfortable in and then attend regularly.
- If one of you is further along spiritually, never laugh at questions or comments your partner might make.
- Participate in a Bible study or class that you both are interested in, so you are learning together.
- When making decisions, ask together, "What would God want us to do?" Then follow His promptings.

Chapter 5: COMMITMENT

You have expressed a commitment to your relationship if you are reading these words. The last broad area of your relationship has to do with some very practical parts of your life. The umbrella that the sub points are listed under is "commitment"

Making a commitment can be a hard thing. Basically, you are making a promise that extends into the future. None of us knows what the future may bring so making a commitment requires a great deal of faith.

The reason this is the last broad category in the tool Live Happily Ever After is because faith becomes easier when we become more experienced. Through these pages we've talked about the major areas that can successfully build a committed relationship. The more you have learned and put into practice, the easier it is to have faith in your future.

I remember when Lynne and I bought our first house. We were very poor but owning was actually cheaper than renting. I remember going over the paperwork with the lending company and promising to pay for the next 30 years. I was only 27 at the time, so I approached signing those papers with a lot of fear. I kept thinking "What if I get sick?" "What if I have unexpected bills?" "What happens if one of our children has special needs?" The list that went through my mind seemed endless.

There I was sitting, pen in hand and the loan officer asked if there was a problem. I pretended that there wasn't, but inside I was a mess. Making commitments that are to last longer than you have lived is a big deal.

When you begin a relationship, you may experience some commitment phobia. You may struggle having confidence in your future. I can understand all of the reasons why people want to minimize risk in a relationship. What many don't realize is by limiting risk, you are also limiting reward. A relationship can never reach its full potential if you set limits. You will become a serial dater for the rest of your life if you aren't willing to take the risk to define your relationship. To me, the best way to do that is marriage.

In the remaining part of this book we will discuss the sub areas of reaching a place you want to make a commitment in your relationship.

By the way. The mortgage that was so hard to sign we had only for 3 years and then we moved. From the sale of the house we made enough money to make a down payment on another house. That mortgage was a bit easier to sign. Over the years, we have moved and purchased seven homes. Each mortgage was easier to sign and had I never gotten the courage to sign the first mortgage we would still be renting rather than having our house paid off.

Share Core Values

When people first date they focus on what they have in common. As a relationship progresses hard conversations have to be discussed about what you each want out of life.

When those conversations begin you may decide that your preferred futures are totally different and although it may have been fun dating, it would be a terrible mistake for you to get married.

Some people get married knowing that they don't have shared values believing that they can change the other person. These relationships are usually filled with arguments because they don't share the same world view or goals.

Have you ever taken the time to think about your core values? You have them whether you realize it or not. You have to begin by asking yourself questions about what is important to you and what you believe to be true. Some areas might be undecided, but eventually you will make a judgment on that subject as well.

Your values are like a compass that can guide you when you feel lost. If your partner has a compass that points to a different direction, you will never know which way to go.

Dating can be a lot of fun. Usually with lots of activities and small talk. Eventually, you have to move on from small talk and decide what you believe about things and share those. Where there are political, philosophical or spiritual differences it becomes much harder to develop true intimacy.

I've talked to couples that believe very different things in areas of core values and the way they work it out is to never talk about those subjects. That is not a solution.

During the course of getting to know one another ask questions about each other. Ask your partner about his or her past, future goals, and beliefs. Continue to ask yourself if there is value alignment. No matter how attractive that person might be to you, if you don't have shared values it will never work.

A couple made a pre-marital appointment with me. When they came to my office the woman held out her left hand and showed me her beautiful engagement ring. I congratulated them and then they asked me if I would officiate at their wedding. I got to know them better, agreed, and put it on my calendar.

We started our pre-marriage counseling and we had a wonderful time. They truly were a wonderful couple. Early on I talked to them about children. He was a bit older than she was and they both said that they didn't plan on becoming parents. Toward the end of our sessions I would always loop back and make sure that they hadn't changed their minds about anything. I reminded them that they told me they didn't want to have children. He quickly agreed and she paused. The wedding was two weeks away, so I asked her if she had changed her mind. She started to cry and shared that she loved her fiancé so much that she wanted to marry him even though she had a huge desire to have a family. She had never told him. She was hoping that he would change his mind.

This was shocking to him and I asked him again, do you want to be a father? He said "No." I explained to the woman that no one can force a person to become a parent. We sat quietly for a few moments and then I asked her if this was a "deal breaker" and she said yes. She couldn't imagine her life without children.

This is a great case where there wasn't value alignment. The good news is several years later she once again came into my office with her left hand leading the way in. I once again said congratulations. I met her new fiancé and learned about their relationship and before I could ask, she blurted out, "He wants a big family!" I was so happy when the day came for them to get married. We had talked through every possible issue and then looped back around, and they were totally ready to get married.

Today, she is the mother of five children, and they are great parents but even better spouses. This is the importance of value alignment.

Helpful Hints:

- Discuss what your values are without judgment. If they are far apart and the results are affecting your relationship, find a neutral third party to help you work things through. If the issue can't be resolved, then it's better to end the relationship.

- Make decisions prior to marriage about the priorities in your lives and make sure they substantially overlap.

- If you plan on having children, make sure that you can speak for each other and will back each other up. Being parents adds a big challenge to any relationship, but it is wonderful if you are prepared.

- If you are concerned about your partner's behavior or beliefs talk to them about it. If they are true convictions, they are unlikely to change. You have to decide how strong your opinions are before you move to a deeper commitment.

Financial Stability

The two most common areas that couple fight about are sex and money.

We just talked about core values, or what's really important to you. What you value is usually where you spend your money. If you don't share the same values, then you will argue all the time about how you spend your money.

Very few people today are financially literate. I have found that during pre-marriage sessions I would teach a class on basic financial principles. If you don't know this information you will always feel financial stress. If you understand the rules of compounding interest, long-term investment and living under your means, you are likely to never have a fight about money.

Prior to Lynne and I getting married a couple asked us over for dinner. They said that in their early days of marriage they were always fighting about money until they learned a secret and since then they have never fought about money. They asked us if we wanted to know about it. We said in unison "YES!" They were a couple with a strong faith, and they wanted their faith to direct their finances. They said if you follow these five steps you won't ever have a fight about your finances. We listened and we have never had an argument in 42 years about how we would spend our money.

This is what we were taught:

1) First give to God. People have different opinions about what percent to give, but they told us to make that our first priority.

2) Pay your bills. They defined bills as monthly expenses which did not include credit cards. They said you'll never have enough money to pay for yesterday and today, so don't buy anything with a credit card unless you are sure you can pay if off at the end of the month. To this day we have never paid a penny of interest on a credit card. They advised us to never buy a car without a significant down payment and the ability to pay if off in three years. They told us to continue to drive the car and save what the payment was and try to pay cash for your next car. We followed their advice and bought modest vehicles and saved the money after the car was paid off. It took us 15 years of marriage and since then we only bought a car we could pay cash for. Each month we put aside money for a future car.

3) Save 10% of your gross income. Our income has never been very large, but at 21 years old we followed this couple's advice.

We started retirement accounts very young that have grown to a place that we are financially secure. I share with every couple I counsel with. Some take the advice and others don't. Retirement comes quickly. I'm 63 and Lynne is 61 and we are fortunate to have taken care of our retirement needs. I actually think we will earn more in retirement than we did while we were working.

4) Bless others. We were taught that after first giving to God, paying our bills and saving 10% of our money we were to be generous with others. There are many people with needs, and we built money into our budget to help others. This category has grown to a much larger amount because we have no debt and our retirement has been secured. We have also had a heart to give to those who are always giving to others. We had a close friend who was a physician. He worked very hard and made a good salary but was far from rich. He told me that whenever he went out to eat with a couple and the check came, they waited

for him to pay. I felt so terrible. I made sure that we expressed generosity back to them and we grew very close. They knew we wanted nothing from them but their friendship.

5) Bless yourself. It took quite a number of years before there was any money that fell into this category. When it did, we bought memories through shared experiences and adventures with our family. When we moved to a different house, we always made sure that any upgrade in housing was based on this category.

The couple that shared this plan with us will never know how much this helped us. If any couple at any income level chose to live by these values, there would never be a need to argue.

There was one Christmas that I asked Lynne if there was anything special, I could buy her. She said she didn't need anything. Lynne is a beautiful woman inside and out and loves bargains. She shops at Good Will and today takes our grandson Ford out on dates where they go to Good Will to look for treasures and then out for ice-cream. He loves it.

That Christmas I decided to give Lynne an envelope with ten $100-dollar bills in it. We had that it the "Bless others" account. I told her to take the month of December and find people she felt led to bless. She told me that it was the best gift she had ever received. We were only able to do that and so many things because we followed the advice of the couple that invited us to dinner one evening.

Helpful Hints:

- Begin using the five steps of financial management listed above.
- Go over the budget together whenever you pay the bills.
- If you are in debt, get help from a financial planner and work together to solve the problem. This will ease the stress in the household immensely.
- If possible, make sure you both have a little fun money to use at your discretion.

- Encourage your partner with something they would like. Don't go in debt to do this.
- Before you go out and spend a large amount of money, make sure your partner agrees.
- If one partner stays at home and does not financially contribute to the family, remember that they still play an integral part to the well-being of the household and likely work much harder than if they took a position in a company. Make sure that you appreciate all they do. They have more than a fulltime job.
- Develop a long-term financial plan that allows for retirement.
- Make sure you have adequate life insurance to provide security for your family.

Ability to Handle Aversity.

Life is challenging to all of us. Sometimes we forget looking back how hard it was when we got started. There are so many adjustments to make and often, if we are young, we are low on money and have big expenses ahead. This is reality for most everyone, so we have to learn to go with the flow and find our greatest pleasure in the committed relationship we have.

As we move on in life there are always unexpected challenges that have to be dealt with. If your primary goal is to keep your marriage in a great place, then you will be able, as a team to handle these hard times.

Lynne and I experienced poverty, just like everyone does. We expected it, so we just worked the plan from the previous section on financial management.

We had babies that would cry most of the night and we would wonder how we could make it through the day.

We both went through long academic programs completing college and graduate school.

We weren't prepared for what came next. Our oldest son, who we loved with all our hearts started to experiment with drugs. We had absolutely no idea that this had happened or was even possible. They day we learned about it, we were terrified. For a year he had friends who experimented, but for our son it was different. He became an addict. He was just 14 years old and we tried everything we possibly could, but nothing we did helped. We lived in fear for his life for 13 years until we received a phone call that he had over dosed and died. We were living in Orlando at the time and quickly made arrangements to travel back to Oshkosh Wisconsin. The evening before the flight Lynne and I talked and we said that we didn't know what our future was, but our only goal was to stay married.

An extremely high percentage of couples that lose a child get divorced. It's a combination of blaming yourself and blaming your spouse. Lynne could have been mother of the year, even during all these years our son heard us tell him of our love for him daily. The last message that was on his phone was me calling to check in with him and I ended by telling him how much I loved him. The police officer that listened to his messages told me that I was leaving the message at about the time of his death.

Addiction is a terrible thing. My father died of alcoholism at just 46 years of life. I do believe that there are some genetic factors in who becomes addicted and who doesn't. I had a terrible time dealing with the grief that followed our son's death. My only goal was to keep our marriage intact. This was not a time of prospering, but a time of surviving through each day that followed.

My reaction to all of this was anxiety and at one point I went to the hospital thinking I was having a heart attack. It took six months to find the right doctor, but that man saved me from such a dark place.

My wife's reaction was depression. She too found help from the same doctor who showed such kindness to us.

It's now been 14 years ago that he died and the previous 13 years before that we feared for his safety. He was a really good kid if you removed the drugs. The night that he died he was talking to other addicts about his relationship with God and how he was praying for help. We believe that God had mercy on him and took him to heaven.

We live in a time of unprecedented drug dependency. I only wish that we could have somehow stopped him from making those decisions.

Over these 14 years, each year has gotten a bit easier. There isn't a day that goes by that we don't think about him. He has a daughter, that we love so much and has turned out to be the best of all of his qualities. She is graduating from college this year with a high-grade point average and has gotten married to a wonderful man. I know her future will be very bright.

The talk we had the evening our son died was to simplify all of our life goals to one; that our marriage would survive. It did survive and even prospered. We relied on each other to gain the strength to make it through the day.

I hope you never have to suffer the loss of a child. But I know you will face adversity. If you have followed the instructions in this book and measured your growth using the tool Live Happily Ever After, you will grow through adversity. Your love will grow deeper, and you will value each other more than ever before.

God has blessed us even through this adversity. We have our beautiful granddaughter, Arianna and her husband, Ben. We also have one biological son who has a beautiful bride and two children. They are doing so well. We are so proud of David and Becca, Ford and River.

We still had excess love to give and God expanded our family by bringing adults that wanted to join our family. Our family has grown to include the following who have added great meaning to our lives: Rahul and Shaloo Kumar and our grandson Viaan Bryan Carter, and Robert Arthur.

We asked our son David how he felt about our family expansion and he told us that if he adopted a child, we would be their grandparents. He welcomed each of his new siblings with open arms.

Someday I might write a book about how God has pieced together out of our weakness a wonderful family that has withstood adversity. We are Swedish, African American, Indian and German all wrapped together in what one day heaven will look like. We feel so blessed to have each of these people in our life. We love them and feel great love from them.

Helpful Hints:

- Look at challenging times as an opportunity to demonstrate your love for your partner.
- Remember that everyone (including you) have made and will make mistakes.
- If you make a mistake that hurt your partner go to them, take responsibility and ask for forgiveness. They may not be able to offer forgiveness that moment. Allow them to process the information and wait for their response.
- If your partner has made a decision or behaved in a way that adversely affected you, talk with them about what happened and offer your forgiveness. This means you don't bring it up any more.
- There are many types of adversity. Many have nothing to do with your partner. If the adversities are frustrating to you, be

careful not to take it out on your partner. Set aside some time to talk through your situation and together work on a solution. Remind each other of your long-term commitment to each other.

Final Word

If you are reading this book, you have heard my story and why I wrote the tool Live Happily Ever After. I truly believe that we can live a rich life filled with love that first begins with God and then the person we give our life to. I don't think a person is "lucky" to have a good marriage. I think they are wise. Wherever you are now in your relationship, I would like to encourage you to take Live Happily Ever After every six months and when you get the results focus on an area or two. The next time you take it you will see your progress. I know that this tool works because it has worked for Lynne and me.

Pastors and Counselors

If you are a Counselor or a Pastor, I hope you will find the tool helpful. There are reports made available only to certified Counselors or Pastors. Please use this tool to help prepare couples for marriage or to improve their relationship. We trust that you are capable of working well with people, but you do need to set up an account for professionals doing relationship counseling. You can go to the website www.livehappilyeverafter.com and click on the box for Counselors or Pastors. There is a small fee to set up the account that will allow you to access all past reports from couples you have invested in and some additional reports that will help you gain greater clarity to what the couple you are working with is experiencing. This is only available to you as a Counselor or a Pastor. Our greatest desire is to help you serve those who come to you. Please forward any suggestion on how we can improve this tool to info@livehappilyeverafter.com.

Made in the USA
Coppell, TX
25 January 2021